CRAPPED OUT

How Gambling Ruins the Economy and Destroys Lives

Edited by
Jennifer Vogel

Common Courage Press   **Monroe, Maine**

Library of Congress Cataloging-in-Publication Data
Vogel, Jennifer.
Crapped out: how gambling ruins the economy and destroys
lives/Jennifer Vogel.
p. cm.
Includes index
ISBN 1-56751-12-X. —ISBN 1-56751-120-1 (pbk.)
1. Gambling—United States. I. Title.
HV6715.V67 1997
363.4'2'0973—dc21   96-39949
CIP

All articles reprinted with permission of the publication listed
with the author byline.

Common Courage Press
Box 702
Monroe, ME 04951

207-525-0900   fax: 207-525-3068

First Printing

This book would not have been possible without the editing skills, researching chops and kindness and support of my family, co-workers and friends. Special thanks go to Mary Ellen Egan, Pete Hilgendorf, Elizabeth Larsen, Steve Perry, and Britt Robson. You guys are great.

Contents

Part I

From Social Ill to Social Will
Gambling Goes Legit

Part II

States Roll the Dice
Betting on the Economy

Part III

The Selling of the Lottery
Promises to the People

Part IV

Corruption, Lawbreaking and the Mob
Just Like Old Times

Part V

Taking the Saps
Advertising and Other Tricks of the Trade

Part VI

Picking Shallow Pockets

Part VII

Over the Edge
The Cost of Compulsive Gambling

Introduction

Disneyland With Dice:
Cannibalizing the Economy
Under the Guise of Entertainment

In 1995, Americans spent more on gambling than the U.S. government budgeted for defense: around $500 billion in all, or $2,000 for every man, woman and child. From lottery tickets at the corner store to slot machines in a Las Vegas casino, more was spent on gambling than on movies, sporting events, concerts or theater. Large-scale casinos have cropped up from coast to coast: before 1989, they were legal only in Nevada and New Jersey, while 27 states now have them. There are pulltabs and other less blatant forms of gambling in bars and restaurants, lotteries on the Internet, and "video gaming" machines on international flights. Thirty-seven states now operate lotteries, up from a handful just 15 years ago. All told, some form of gambling now operates in every state except Hawaii and Utah. It's clear that gambling has become America's fastest growing industry.

"For the first time," brags a 1996 brochure from Harrah's Entertainment Inc., "more than half of the nation's states each generate more than 1 million household casino trips per year...U.S. households made 154 million visits to casinos in 1995, an increase of 23 percent over the previous year and 235 percent over 1990." The pamphlet goes on to claim that states are benefiting from gambling in terms of job creation and new taxes. Gambling proponents and many politicians would have the public believe that casinos and lotteries are harmless and voluntary fun, doing nothing but economic and social good for the communities that host them. It's often claimed—especially around the time the matter is up for public vote—that a lottery will increase education or environmental spending, that a casino will revitalize a sluggish economy. In fact, these promises often don't come true; in many cases, gambling only makes a bad situation worse. In Texas, elected officials claimed that a lottery would keep taxes down. Citizens, predictably, voted for a lottery and ended up with a hearty tax hike anyway. Gambling itself has enormous hidden costs: increased compulsive gambling, bankruptcies, crime, small business closings. Casinos came to Atlantic City in 1978, but they haven't revitalized the slumping economy there. Retail businesses have closed in droves, replaced by pawnshops. Unemployment has risen. As law professor and gambling expert I. Nelson Rose once told *U.S. News & World Report*: "Atlantic City used to be a slum by the sea. Now it's a slum by the sea with casinos."

The first modern-day casinos opened in Reno, Nevada, in the 1930s, just after the state passed laws legalizing gambling and making it easier to obtain a divorce. The legislation was big news all over America. "Nevada is tired of cactus, alkali wastes, sparse population, hard times and virtue," reported Alabama's *Montgomery Advertiser* at the time. Despite criticism, a new gambling Mecca, Las Vegas, blossomed in the desert throughout the late '40s and early '50s, creating a new world of nonstop dreams and sparkling lights that bore very little resemblance to everyday America. It was constructed by mobsters and other questionable characters like Bugsy Siegel and Lester "Benny" Binion, who left the illegal casino business in Dallas for Nevada legitimacy in a Cadillac packed with suitcases of cash.

Atlantic City contested Nevada's gambling monopoly in 1978, providing the first experiment at bringing casinos into an existing city for the purpose of economic revitalization. Since then, casinos have appeared in places like Black Hawk, Colorado, and Deadwood, South Dakota. Paddleboat casinos, designed to circumvent state laws banning land-based casinos, chug up and down the Mississippi River, stopping at ports in Iowa, Illinois and Mississippi. The Indian Gaming Regulatory Act of 1988 provided Native Americans the right to conduct for profit any form of gambling that states put on for charity. Suddenly, church basement "Las Vegas Nights" became full-fledged 24-hour, tribal-run casinos. Today, they make up only a small part of the overall gambling picture, despite the disproportionate amount of publicity they garner. According to a 1996 issue of *U.S. News & World Report*, non-reservation casinos took in $367.9 billion in bets in 1994, while reservation gambling halls took in only $41.1 billion. Meanwhile, lottery gambling has spread wildly across the country, starting in 1964 with New Hampshire. Thirty years later, all but 12 states were running them, taking in $34.5 billion in wagers.

Gambling's proliferation is, in part, due to its new, more palatable image. Gone are the days of overt mob-control—though examples of involvement in casino management and contracting persist. Today, the Flamingo hotel that Siegel built is owned by the Hilton Hotels Corporation and is traded on the stock market. As David Johnston describes in his book *Temples of Chance*, excerpted later in this book: "In 1989 there were 1,589 Holiday Inns in America. But the Holiday Corporation earned 28 cents of each dollar's profit from a single building in Atlantic City—Harrah's Marina Hotel Casino." Gambling, said one industry executive recently, "has gone through cycles of being prohibited and legalized. But now, for the first time, it is being legitimized. It's coming into the American mainstream."

Powerful investors such as Donald Trump, Merv Griffin and Steve Wynn have done their part to make casinos appear to be good, clean fun. They've built fantasy lands and Ozs with volcanoes, rollercoasters and huge fountains. The strategy today is to attract working class families or "lowrollers." According to a November 1993 issue of *Institutional Investor* magazine, the trend is especially prevalent in Las Vegas, which has found itself competing with casinos across the country: "Mirage Resorts has built a moat and has begun to stage pirate battles. Circus Circus recently opened its 30-story pyramid in the desert. The MGM Grand is putting up a billion-dollar sphinxlike edifice that it boasts will be 'the largest casino in the galaxy' in 'the world's largest hotel.' The Hilton, meanwhile, is erecting a monstrous, 363-foot structure that manager F.M. (Bud) Celey declares will be 'the worlds biggest sign'...The aim in Vegas, once 'sin city', is to create a continuous carnival of spectacles, a 'destination resort' for the whole family. The new Vegas wants to be Disneyland with dice."

That comparison is especially appropriate since staking the future on gambling, economists argue, could only work in a fantasyland. It's an industry that produces no product and no new wealth, and thus makes no genuine contribution to economic development. "Governmental officials are increasingly being enticed to accept and then impose upon the public those discredited economic philosophies which claim that gambling activities increase jobs, foster economic development, and generate new tax revenues—all without raising taxes on the electorate," says University of Illinois economist John Warren Kindt. "In reality, the regional and strategic impacts of legalized gambling almost invariably result in a net loss of jobs, increased taxes, and negative economic spiral which is inherently recessionary...Furthermore, the net creation of jobs claimed by the legalized gambling industry is at best a break-even proposition, and the evidence suggests that net job losses can easily occur—primarily because 'consumer dollars' are drained from the rest of the economy. The literature frequently refers to this process as 'cannibalization.'"

Even some of those who seek to win by running the industry have lost their shirts. According to a March 1992 piece in *Washington Monthly* magazine, the Seneca-Cayuga Indians in Oklahoma hired Wayne Newton Enterprises in October 1990 to run a high-stakes bingo parlor. The tribe had shelled out $300,000 to build the hall and was asked for another $224,000 to get the operation up and running, while Newton was to contribute a never-to-materialize $125,000. By the end of 1991, ledgers reported gross earnings of $12.5 million for the year, yet the parlor recorded a debt of $360,000, which Newton wanted the tribe to pay. Angry tribe members finally gained control of the operation after surrounding the hall with pick-up trucks while Newton's security forces barricaded themselves inside. Though this book doesn't discuss issues specific to Indian gambling, such as sovereignty, various reports have shown that they face the same problems as other communities when it comes to corruption and social costs. "Wherever it's been tried," the *Washington Monthly* article says, "gambling has been accompanied by a dramatic increase in violent and property crimes, alcoholism, and drug abuse."

Tom Grey, head of the National Coalition Against Legalized Gambling, has become the anointed leader of America's swelling anti-gambling movement. A Methodist minister from Hanover, Illinois, Grey discovered back in 1991 that the local county board had approved docking rights to a riverboat casino without consulting the public. "I remember thinking, what a dumb idea," he says. "Gambling is gambling. It's not the kind of activity you bring into a small rural, conservative community. I thought, gambling makes losers." He discovered that others—housewives, artists—felt the same way. "We invited a state's attorney from Deadwood in for two town meetings. We figured we ought to know what we were getting into. He told us that he wasn't against gambling but that we should be aware that they had wanted only four casinos that would operate during the off season, to maintain a tourist base. He said they wound up with 80 casinos running year round. He said that three car dealerships had closed up. You could have heard a pin drop in that auditorium." Grey and his supporters gathered enough signatures to put the matter on a public ballot, and even though he says casino interests spent $30,000 to counter the campaign, the 21,000 citizens of JoDaviess County voted the proposal down by a huge margin. The vote, it turned out, wasn't enough to convince the state, which approved the necessary licensing anyway. Grey's been fighting gambling ever since, traveling the country organizing and giving speeches.

Grey's efforts, along with the persistence of gambling-related problems, has had an impact on the public consciousness. Casino proliferation slowed to a trickle in 1994 and stringent community opposition to gambling has occurred in a number of locales where expansion was planned. In addition—at the prompting of NCALG—Congress recently passed a bill mandating a national study of the social and economic effects of gambling. (The last such federal study was over 20 years ago, in 1976.) The battle was hard won; the gambling industry reportedly spent millions lobbying against the proposal. But legislators like then-Senator Paul Simon, who co-authored the legislation, made strong arguments. In a July 1995 speech before the Senate, he explained the crucial importance of a large-scale study of "our fastest growing industry." "The gambling elite are not only generous employers of lobbyists, they are multi-million dollar donors to political campaigns, and the combination makes them politically potent," he said. "The unsavory and unhealthy influence of lobbyists and legislators as protectors of this rapidly growing industry means sensible restraint will not be easily achieved." The commission—which will comprise nine appointed members and will have two years to come up with findings—will review gambling policies on a federal, state, local and tribal level and will study gambling's relationship to issues like crime and pathological gambling. It will look at how much money states and tribes make from gambling and explore alternative revenue sources.

Many of the issues and viewpoints the commission will undoubtedly focus on are detailed in this book, which contains articles from a wide variety of publications. They paint a grim picture, one that the gambling industry would rather nobody sees. Aside from discussing compulsive gambling, bankruptcies, increased crime, ongoing mob ties, political corruption and manipulative advertising strategies, these articles illustrate that although casinos and lotteries may provide some short-term economic benefits for hard-pressed states and reservations, in the long run they do more harm than good. Kindt estimates that for every dollar gambling contributes in taxes, taxpayers spend at least three dollars on everything from fixing up streets around casinos to increasing police patrols and treating pathological gamblers. The number of compulsive gamblers has been shown to increase in states with legalized gambling, sometimes by 500 percent; the average social cost of a compulsive gambler is estimated to be as high as $53,000 per year.

It's obvious that no matter who is running a casino or a lottery, the issues are the same—a few people get rich while draining money from the rest. Gambling undercuts real economic development, critics point out again and again, while placing citizens' heads on the chopping block.

What are the odds that the gambling movement will be pushed back in favor of meaningful economic activity? Community opposition—along with the often predicted saturation of the market—has the gambling industry on the defensive already. In 1995 it set up the American Gaming Association with the express mission of "creating a better understanding of gaming-entertainment by bringing the facts about the industry to the general public." The AGA's media packet includes a pamphlet called "Gaming Industry Myths and Facts," which refers to gambling as "one of the greatest contributors to our nation's economy" and frets over the fact that "critics still perpetuate old stereotypes." In the end, whether gambling lives or dies will depend heavily on citizen action.

Part I
From Social Ill to Social Will
Gambling Goes Legit

Nearly every time gambling has taken hold in this country, public outcry over the inevitable corruption that surrounds it has driven it back. One of the most dramatic and oft-cited examples of citizens taking matters into their own hands happened in Vicksburg, Mississippi, in 1835. Riverboat gamblers, or "blacklegs" as they were unceremoniously called in those days, operated in shabby gambling houses throughout the city until townsfolk, tired of being ripped off, decided to settle the score. A group of vigilantes took to the street, ransacking the gambling establishments and busting up anything that got in their way. When five gamblers tried to hide, they were hunted down and hanged.

Today the relationship between the public and gambling institutions is much cozier. Gambling has been allowed to weave its way into American culture in an unprecedented fashion. It's become as legitimate as Disneyworld, as commonplace as an electronics superstore—just another form of consumer entertainment controlled by big business interests. No longer do gamblers operate in tucked-away shacks; they serve free cocktails and cheap buffet lunches in fancy palaces. Gambling has expanded dramatically under its new management; today's moguls have more to spend on advertising, lush accommodations and political support than mobsters ever did.

Politicians can now associate themselves with gambling and not expect to lose many votes; it's a relationship that benefits everyone but the public. The gambling industry lobbies hard and makes giant political contributions (see the tables at the end of this chapter) to both parties. According to "Vegas Bob," an editorial in the February 12, 1996, issue of the *Nation*, "*Casino*, the movie, hasn't made much money for Martin Scorsese. But casino, the fundraiser, has been working wonders for Bob Dole. Not long ago, Las Vegas mogul Steve Wynn, C.E.O. of Mirage Resorts, raised $478,000 for Dole's presidential campaign at a single event...Dole's Las Vegas godfathers are paying the Senator for services rendered in 1993, when he killed President Clinton's proposal for a 4 percent tax on gambling revenues to pay for health care and welfare reform." Gambling has made a remarkable transition, and politicians are going along for the ride.

America Inc.
Buys Out Murder Inc.

David Johnston
Excerpted from *Temples of Chance*, Doubleday, 1992

Since the dashing Bugsy Siegel built America's first gambling resort, the Flamingo, in 1946, mobsters and murder have shaped the desolate stretch of asphalt known as South Las Vegas Boulevard into the pulsating neon forest known around the world as the Strip. The idea that Las Vegas is a Mafia-run playground, and that Atlantic City is the Mafia's empire in the East, contains powerful romantic appeal. *The Godfather* and a thousand other movies, novels and television shows have burned into the public consciousness the image of casino gambling as a mob business.

That image no longer reflects reality.

Today the Flamingo is owned by Hilton Hotels Corporation, a Fortune Service 500 company traded on the New York Stock Exchange (NYSE). Next door, at the corner of the Strip and Dunes Boulevard, stands the Barbary Coast, whose investors include Richard Crane, former chief of the U.S. Justice Department Organized Crime Strike Force in Los Angeles, which prosecutes Vegas mobsters. Across Dunes Boulevard from the Barbary Coast is Bally's Las Vegas. It opened as the MGM Grand and then, after a disastrous 1980 fire that killed eighty-four people, was acquired by Bally Manufacturing, another NYSE company. Catty-corner from Bally's Las Vegas and across the Strip from the Flamingo, Roman statuary guards a grand oval reflecting pool bordered by streams of cool water cascading into the desert air. This ancient imperial setting encompasses Caesar's Palace, the casino most associated with mobsters in films. Money from the then-mob-dominated Teamsters union built this pleasure dome in 1966, but today its stock also trades on the NYSE. Its chief executive's office, a dice throw from Beverly Hills, has not been occupied by a mob associate for more than a decade.

Next to Caesars, behind a tropical lagoon dotted with palm trees and a volcano that shoots steam and flames in the night air, stands the most ostentatious gambling palace of them all, Steve Wynn's Mirage, which opened on Thanksgiving weekend 1989. Mirage Resorts' stock trades on the Big Board, too. Across the street from the Mirage, next to Hilton's Flamingo, sits the giant riverboat facade of Harrah's (until recently called the Holiday casino). It was once owned by a company that became a household name by catering to middle-class American families on vacation, the Holiday Inn chain based in Memphis, Tennessee. The stock of Holiday and its successor firm, the Promus Companies, also trade on the NYSE.

Ramada Inn bought the Tropicana in 1979—twenty-two years after that casino opened as a mob joint.

Across the Strip from the Trop a gargantuan white version of a medieval castle with bright red-and-blue spires rose in 1990. The Excalibur is the world's largest hotel, with four thousand budget rooms and a two-and-a-half-acre casino designed on a Knights of the Round Table theme. Excalibur is owned by Circus Circus, a New York Stock Exchange company so well-managed that every third dollar in revenues flows directly into its treasury.

On the third corner at South Las Vegas and Tropicana Boulevard, investors are backing the building of an even larger casino resort, the five-thousand-room MGM, which will adjoin a theme park filled with rides and amusements inspired by the classic 1939 MGM film The Wizard of Oz. The fourth corner is owned by a Japanese firm that builds slot machines. In time another giant casino is sure to rise from this sand-swept place.

Fly east to Atlantic City and the story is similar. Hilton, Holiday and Ramada all came here, although Hilton had to sell out to Donald Trump when it was refused a New Jersey casino license in 1985 because of past mob ties that the company refused to confess. (Hilton tried again and easily won a New Jersey license in 1991.)

Caesars is in Atlantic City, too. Bally has two Boardwalk casinos, one of them purchased from Steve Wynn's company at a fantastically inflated price when he retreated to the desert to create his Mirage.

The Atlantic City market is dominated, though, by Donald Trump. He owns three of the area's twelve casinos and controlled Resorts, the first Boardwalk gambling hall, until Merv Griffin bought it in a hostile takeover that grew from stock market manipulation. Shares of two Trump casinos and Resorts trade on the American Stock Exhange, as do the bonds of all four casinos.

Of the dozen casinos in Atlantic City all but one has publicly traded stock or bonds. A complex partnership owns the exception, the Claridge, which until 1989 had been the property of a publicly traded company with an interesting tie to the history of modern Las Vegas: the old owner was the Del E. Webb Corp., which built the Flamingo for Bugsy Siegel.

The individual gamblers and their underworld backers who built Las Vegas, and who escaped both jail and hitmen, began selling out two decades ago, replaced by a new generation of owners: corporations specializing in the business of risk. In the casino industry, America Inc. bought out Murder Inc.

Brand name hotel chains—Hilton, Holiday, Ramada—moved into the gambling business in the seventies. Meanwhile, New Jersey casino regulators forced men tainted by dealings with mobsters to resign as the chief executives of Bally Manufacturing and Caesars. These five firms plus Wynn's Mirage, Circus Circus and Trump dominate the casino business in America today.

The gambling boom that rebuilt the Atlantic City Boardwalk and launched a new era on the Strip in Las Vegas was not limited to America, but was part of a global phenomenon. From Moscow to Sidney, from Saipan to Warsaw, and from Cairo to Aruba investors poured money into new temples of chance designed to attract the prospering multitudes to their games.

Just as Bugsy Siegel saw the potential for Las Vegas in the prosperity that was sure to follow the Second World War, in the seventies and eighties the corporate executives who ran the megascasinos in Nevada and New Jersey began envisioning the potential for a global gambling market. Their most intensive missionary work was reserved for those who had access to millions or even tens of millions of dollars and were driven by the desire to advance into the realm of high rollers.

Australia, whose government envied the growing riches of Japan (where casino wagering is forbidden) started casinos aimed at Asian tourists and invited Harrah's Pratt Hotel and others to bid for licenses. In Canada entrepreneurs devised the most ambitious gambling plan ever, a global lottery whose prize was an annuity that would pay out $1 billion, an idea whose success awaits only government approvals. Carnival Cruise Lines showed its competitors how to fatten profit margins by adding a few blackjack and roulette tables and some slot machines to help vacationers while away the hours just as passengers had on Mississippi paddle wheelers a century and a half earlier.

During the eighties corporate gamblers applied mass merchandising techniques to give betting a new image, although the underlying reality remained unchanged. The basic human desires that make gambling appealing to most people still stir the blood, but with help from master advertising men—one of whom went on to mold President Bush's image in the White House—these gaming corporations successfully repackaged the popular view of gambling, selling it as just another form of recreation by making it appear to be free of either moral or financial worries.

Their success selling gambling as entertainment, as a fun way to pass an evening or a week, holds important consequences for the nation's economic future because it ignores the potential for ruin and how the casinos encourage that outcome. Casino marketers direct attention away from the psychological pull that makes some players into compulsive gamblers who will steal to play and many more into obsessives who plunk every spare quarter into the slots. Unlike cocaine or Disneyland, which can be consumed only until exhaustion sets in, there is no limit to how much a gambler can lose in a single sitting.

The level of betting practiced regularly by high rollers today was never allowed when mobsters controlled the casino business in Nevada. The mob lacked the bankroll to pay out winnings that might reach a million bucks in five minutes. Then casinos were run by men who learned casino management on the streets and who relied on the crude method of skimming casino winnings in the count room to make their operations worthwhile.

They have been succeeded by college graduates expert at handling money. Today's casino companies are run by graduates of Harvard, Cornell and Penn's Wharton School of Finance. These executives earn extraordinary sums even in the context of the bloated salaries of corporate America. Former stockbroker Richard Gillman, who runs Bally's four casinos, earned a base pay of $4 million for years and in 1988 was paid more than $10 million. (His name did not appear in the business magazine lists of well paid CEOs, however, because he only ran Bally's casino unit.) Dennis Gomes was paid $1.2 million in his first year as president of Donald Trump's Taj Mahal Casino Resort, more than the chief executive of the Ford Motor Company earned. David P. Hanlon earned more than $2 million cash in 1991 to head Merv Griffin's struggling Resorts casinos.

These giant paychecks are possible because the modern hotel-mega-casino generates a torrent of cash, a torrent so huge that it can allow even abysmally managed companies to survive year after disastrous year. A hotel with a casino can net more money *each week* than a plain hotel of similar size might net in a year or even two. Hilton's four Nevada casinos bring in more than twice the revenues of its 264 franchised hotels combined.

Nowhere was the fantastic profitability of well-managed casinos more evident than at the Holiday Corporation. In

1989 there were 1,589 Holiday Inns scattered across the land, yet the Holiday Corporation that year earned twenty-eight cents of each dollar's profit from a single building in a marsh along the New Jersey shore—Harrah's Marina Hotel Casino in Atlantic City. The lure of such phenomenal profits from gambling prompted Holiday management to sell its namesake business in January 1990 to Bass Ale, the British brewers, and to create a new firm devoted to becoming the leading gaming concern in the world. Because it promised to make shareholders and management rich in the nineties and beyond, the new firm was named the Promus Companies.

Ramada quickly followed suit, selling its lodging chain and emerging as a new firm with three big casinos, but saddled with inept management. Barron Hilton tried the same move, but couldn't get a high enough price for the hotel side of the Hilton Hotel Corporation.

These corporate gamblers and others are now investing in lavish fantasy gambling resorts that combine flamboyant design with what the Disney folks—frequent advisors to the casino industry—call *imagineering*. Their aim is to bedazzle customers, creating must-see attractions that will draw millions of new players and keep the old ones coming back.

But fantasy costs money. Wynn's Mirage features the only man-made volcano on earth, a fifty-four-foot cone belching fire and steam every quarter hour after dark. Behind this desert resort dolphins frolic in a seaquarium. The Mirage cost $630 million to build. Circus Circus' Excalibur, with its indoor dinner theater built around a giant dirt ring where knights joust twice nightly, was a comparatively low-budget affair costing $290 million. When completed the new MGM in Las Vegas, with its Oz theme park, will have cost about $1 billion.

Such megacasino projects require access to capital on a scale that the Mafia could not produce even with its influence over the Teamsters union and its profits from drugs, loan-sharking and sweetheart government contracts. The corporate gamblers' friend who made these fantasy palaces possible was Michael Milken of the now bankrupt Drexel Burnham

Lambert securities firm. For years Wynn boasted that Golden Nugget was the first investment banking client Milken brought to Drexel, a boast that lost some of its value after Milken admitted to six felonies and took up residence at the Club Fed an hour's drive from San Francisco.

Milken addicted casino executives to junk, not the kind heroin addicts shoot into their veins in the burned-out buildings a block from the Boardwalk casinos, but the kind companies inject into their books. Junk bonds catapulted Steve Wynn from a mere millionaire to a fortune two hundred times that size, commanding a company with a billion dollars in annual revenue. Hilton, Holiday, Ramada, Circus Circus and Merv Griffin all loaded up on Drexel debt while Donald Trump and others relied on junk sold by Drexel's imitators. Casino companies sold more than $5 billion worth of junk bonds in the eighties, some of which was never paid back despite the supposedly intense regulation of modern casinos by the states of New Jersey and Nevada.

The need for these enormous pools of money to finance megacasinos required the major gaming companies to issue stock and bonds. Today anyone can own part of a casino, occasionally for less money per share than it takes to activate some slot machines. That prosaic fact is not the concept that the casinos want to project, however, to players looking for excitement. The casino companies continue to foster the fiction that mobsters run the joints because an aura of criminality is good for business, appealing to people who would like to rub shoulders with one of John Gotti's henchmen, albeit in a secure environment. Bob Stupak, sole owner of Vegas World (where the Strip begins), believes corporate-owned casinos are bad for business because boring corporate bureaucrats run them. Characters like Benny Binion, who bragged of killing those who crossed him, and Bill Harrah, who in his sixties drag-raced teens at Reno traffic lights, are what the casinos need, he says. Except for himself and Steve Wynn, though, the colorful characters are mostly gone. "What this town needs," Stupak said one night after beating the competing

Aladdin casino's craps table for twenty-four thousand dollars in five minutes, "is that scent of vice, a little sin, to stir that desire to come to Las Vegas."

The godfathers and the wise guys did not just disappear from the casinos when Wall Street arrived. Like many founders leaving a business, they were smart enough to figure out ways to continue getting paid. Mob-connected firms still arrange many gambling junkets, provide buses and limousines, and handle headliners in the showrooms. The result of the continuing involvement of mob figures in lucrative support-ing roles is a dangerous mix of legitimacy and illegitimacy that without aggressive regulation invites scandal, political upheaval and corruption. Casinos remain attractive places to launder illicit cash from cocaine smuggling and insider trading on Wall Street. The mob has discovered rich opportunities in manipulating casino securities.

Today the brand-name companies and others that con-trol the casino industry are busy increasing their market and expanding commercial gambling across the country. Their goal is to make gambling a routine leisure activity for most Americans, as it has become for 28 percent of metropolitan Philadelphia residents—from gritty South Philadelphia row houses as well as the mansions of the Main Line. Among their strategies is encouraging young adults to gamble often—and on credit—as the beer and cigarette companies aim to make customers for life of people just entering adulthood. With their new attractions, from caged tigers to strolling court jesters to a theme park filled with rides, Wynn, Circus Circus, and others are leading a movement to market Las Vegas as a family vacation center, a move that will acquaint legions of little children with the excitement of Las Vegas.

When Nevada had a monopoly on legal American casi-nos, the social and economic problems posed by gambling had a limited impact. Then, in 1978, Atlantic City brought legal casinos to the East Coast; suddenly one in four Americans lived within a six-hour drive of a blackjack table. A decade later South Dakota voters approved gambling in Deadwood.

Play started there in 1990, setting off an explosion of casino gambling. Since then Colorado, Illinois, Iowa, Louisiana and Mississippi have legalized casinos, while gambling halls run by Indians flourish in California, Connecticut, Michigan, Minnesota, Nebraska and Wisconsin.

Indian-owned casinos are likely soon in Florida, Kansas, Nevada, Oklahoma, South Dakota and Washington state. Steve Wynn's Mirage and other experienced casino companies are signing contracts to manage these casinos. The mob has also tried to muscle in on some Indian gaming and at least one Indian leader who spoke out against such involvement was murdered.

Just as significant, and perhaps more so, video slot machines are proliferating, and many in the industry believe they will be a standard feature in nearly every neighborhood tavern in America within a few years. They are already legal along Maryland's Eastern Shore and in Montana, Oregon, South Dakota and West Virginia. Bills to legalize video poker in bars are being pushed aggressively in state capitals across the land, backed not only by the manufacturers, but by public officials who contend that the government cannot adequately police illegal slot machines—so it should license them and share in the profits as way to ease the burdens of taxpayers.

So completely, and quietly, has the trend toward universal casino gambling swept the nation that few people realize that Minnesota now has more casinos than New Jersey. Significantly, one of those is run under an agreement with the city of Duluth, which receives nearly a quarter of the profits from the casino that's housed in an old Sears store. State lottery officials around the nation have closely followed this trend, which started in Canada, and West Virginia has already joined it. More casinos managed or owned by state and local governments are a virtual certainty.

Gambling interests are aggressively pushing for legalization of casino games in a variety of states, including Indiana, Missouri, New York, Pennsylvania and Washington. By 1992, every state but two, Utah and Hawaii, had laws making legal at least one form of commercial gambling: lotteries, casinos, dog or horse racing, jai alai, bingo, sports betting or charity "Las Vegas Nights."

Achieving the gambling industry's goals depends on cooperation from politicians, who must pass laws granting the corporate gamblers exemptions from the criminal statutes governing gambling. In many states approval of gambling occurred only after corporate gamblers and lawmakers joined in promising to funnel the government's cut to specific constituencies, usually senior citizens or public schools.

By the turn of the century half of the states or more will probably have casinos, in part because of a 1987 U.S. Supreme Court decision that recognized the right of Indian tribes to offer any gambling games on their reservations that are allowed in the state where the reservation is located. Thirty-one states allow charities to raise funds through so-called Las Vegas Nights, and fourteen of these states have recognized Indian reservations.

Just outside the little seaport of Mystic, Connecticut, the Mashantucket Pequot Indian tribe's Foxwoods High Stakes Bingo and Casino offers craps, poker, blackjack and other table games, but not slot machines. Within a month of opening, the table drop at Foxwoods—the amount of chips sold—exceeded that at Trump Plaza in Atlantic City. The Pequots plan to add hotels, restaurants and other amenities. Other Indian nations from Nebraska to California are moving to copy all or part of this format, some with professional management.

The gambling companies successfully sold riverboat casinos as the way to polish up Rust Belt centers like Davenport, Iowa, even though they will create few new jobs and may worsen the woes of retailers, as dollars that would have gone to buy toaster and cars, and into a nest egg to supplement pensions, instead are lost at floating craps tables. Some hospitality business chains envision franchising hotels in Old West towns like Deadwood, which before gambling were too small to warrant their attention. In theory gambling is supposed to revive Deadwood as a historic town, the place where Wild Bill Hickock died with two pair, aces and eights, in his hand and a bullet in the back.

Small distant towns like Cripple Creek, Colorado or even Iowa riverports, are not the main interest of the billion-dollar gambling companies like Promus and Mirage Resorts. They want to manage casinos near larger cities like Denver and Omaha. The corporate gamblers also want casinos in the first-class Manhattan hotels, at historic Penn's Landing in Philadelphia, along Pittsburgh's three rivers, in downtown Detroit, and on the lake-front sites of abandoned steel mills in Gary, Indiana, a short drive from the Chicago Loop. In St. Louis and New Orleans and in every other city seeking economic revival, the gambling companies promise new jobs if only legislators will exempt them from laws that make commercial gambling a crime.

As well-paying industrial jobs have begun to dry up in America, the children of the blue-collar workers who once fit truck cabs to frames or cabinets to television sets or, if they were skilled, machined parts on a lathe, are finding gambling tables the nineties' equivalent of the assembly lines where their parents labored. Like their parents they perform repetitive tasks that require little education, such as shuffling cards and passing the dice after a player craps out. The new jobs mean coming home with clean fingernails. They also mean less money, often less than half what their parents made with fewer benefits, little individual job security and no sense that their labor is building anything tangible or enduring. In Atlantic City a side effect has been rising juvenile delinquency, even in the suburbs, with few parents available for weekend activities from organized soccer to church visits.

Casinos were supposed to be the catalyst to rebuild Atlantic City. The promise has never been fulfilled, however, because the law worked against redevelopment by requiring that each temple of chance in Atlantic City be a self-contained city. The main purpose is gambling, but within the temple walls people can dine, drink, exercise, make love and sleep. To tempt those who quit the games while they were ahead, and to keep their winnings from leaving the temple, pricey boutiques offer an array of fancy raiment as well as Tiffany diamonds, Leroy Neiman prints and Kron chocolates.

The casinos are to Atlantic City as factories are to a Third World country, thrown up at a distant location, served by a highway designed primarily to obtain raw materials and ship out finished product. The raw materials coming down the Atlantic City Expressway are wallets and pocket books, which are cleaned of their paper and plastic and then sent back up the highway to be filled again for another trip.

Making full-blown casinos, on land or afloat, easily available to most Americans is just one part of the corporate plan to profit by infecting America with an incurable case of gambling fever. Another gambling company, International Game Technology of Reno, wants to create a vast new market for its video poker machines which allow gamblers to play cards with a computer. IGT wants its high-tech slot machines in every neighborhood bar. But knowing that the term *slot machines* might arouse opposition, the firm relies on the sort of polished sleight of hand long employed by Madison Avenue.

IGT president Charles Mathewson believes there is a market for several hundred thousand of these machines, which differ from casino slots only in that instead of the plink, plink, plink of quarters falling into a metal tray, winners get a slip of paper that the bartender will trade for cash or another shot of bourbon. Because the machines pay winners in scrip, not coin, the gambling industry calls them Video Lottery Terminals or VLTs. The one-armed bandits of the cashless society.

As the nineties began, bills to make slot machines legal began popping up in statehouses like crab grass in spring. "I simply cannot keep track of them all," lamented William R. Eadington, a University of Nevada-Reno economics professor who has been a leader in examining the rise of corporate-owned casinos and the spread of gambling beyond the Silver and Garden states. Sponsors of these slot machine bills argued that the mob earns growing profits from illegal slot machines in bars, many of them fitted with switches so their video screens can change instantly to resemble lawful arcade games.

E.E. "Butch" Brian, the West Virginia lottery director, contends that residents pump $280 million into mob-owned video poker machines, depriving his impoverished Appalachian state of vital revenues. He wants the state government to take over this business, saying it would ease the burdens on taxpayers. In 1990, at Mountaineer Race Track, the West Virginia lottery installed banks of Video Lottery Terminals. After nine months this government-sponsored gambling parlor was producing profits for one of the poorest states in the country, at an annual rate of nearly seven thousand dollars per machine. South Dakota's lottery licensed the same kind of modified slot machines in bars, prompting an immediate 51 percent jump in its lottery revenues.

Some state lottery directors want to go even further than running government-sponsored slot machine parlors. Many of them are looking north to Canada, where in December 1989, the Manitoba Lottery Foundation opened a casino in Winnipeg, a city of six hundred thousand that is just sixty miles north of the Minnesota border. Despite limits on betting it won nearly $20 million from its patrons in the following year.

Eugene Martin Christiansen, a leading gambling industry consultant, watched all the activity taking place to legalize and expand gambling as the nineties began and concluded that "there is a general move toward legal casino-type games. It is part of a fundamental change that is irreversible at this point because the country is changing with fewer people going to church, more older people with time and money on their hands and, especially, with state lottery advertising campaigns that make it seem that buying lottery tickets is almost a patriotic duty."

During the Reagan years Las Vegas shamelessly wrapped itself in the flag, selling itself through national television commercials as "The American Way to Play." Sig Rogich, the veteran Strip publicity agent who coined that phrase, moved on to George Bush's 1988 presidential campaign and then into the White House. President Bush put Rogich in charge of remaking his image from wimp into the brave leader of a New World Order.

As America approaches the dawn of a new millennium, its industrial might withering, the business of chance prospers.

The automobile, steel and electronics industries are in shambles, while legal gambling is one of the country's fastest-growing businesses, touted by politicians as the way to revive dying towns and create jobs. That casinos create no new wealth, that they act to take money from many people and funnel it to the few lucky enough to hold a casino license, seems of little consequence to the growing number of politicians urging more gambling on the public.

Christiansen predicts that between 1989 and 1995 the amount of money Americans lose in casinos will grow by two thirds, from $9 billion to $15 billion. Expand the measure of gambling to include state lotteries—the biggest gambling game of them all—plus horse racing, dog tracks, bingo run by churches and Native Americans as well as legal sports betting, and the total Americans lost gambling legally in 1989 came to $24 billion. Christensen expects that will increase to $40 billion by 1995. Few industries in an era of slow growth or retrenchment can imagine such phenomenal growth, especially for a multibillion-dollar industry whose basic offering is almost as old as mankind's ability to count.

One argument for casinos is that the wise guys continue to shoot the dice at the craps tables. In a perverse way casinos help recycle mob dollars from extortion, loan-sharking and drugs back into the legitimate economy. High rollers generally do not play with money legitimately earned and already taxed by the government. They play with unreported or underreported dollars and in time many of them come to financial ruin or an early death because of their profligacy. Casino owners, too, can run wild with all the cash that comes their way, squandering it instead of using it to expand their businesses or branch out into other economic activities. (Christiansen and others who have studied the industry understand that the financial troubles of Donald Trump's and Merv Griffin's casinos result from borrowing binges and poor management, not from any fundamental weakness in the business of risk.)

Many leaders in the gambling business consider Christiansen's projections conservative, in part because he foresees less government sponsorship than others predict. Flayed by citizens who want additional services from lower taxes, governments now look upon gambling as an easy street for raising money. Pressure to create jobs in areas hardest hit by white-collar layoffs, factory closings and economic decline is spurring more states to approve casinos. Thomas D. Carver, president of the New Jersey Casino Association, believes that the future will include more legal gambling in more places because "government is engaged in a desperate search for ways to raise revenues without raising taxes, and it sees gambling as a painless way to raise money."

Casinos are also engaged in a desperate search for states and cities that will give them just enough regulation to protect them from extortion by organized crime. They want to be otherwise free to run their businesses as they please, to push liquor on a suddenly rich man until he signs away his last penny, to let teenagers play so long as they lose, to borrow money in the securities markets that will never be repaid. They want a double standard in which expendables—dealers, cocktail waitresses, busted high rollers—face severe regulatory actions while owners and executives flout the law and risk nothing more serious than a fine. They want the *appearance* of regulation, and governments desperate for funds are giving it to them.

This growing alliance between the corporate gamblers and politicians is only the latest manifestation of a long history of mutually shared interests between those who understand games of chance and those who exercise political power. Twice before, corruption has brought an end to such alliances. But this third wave of gambling fever is rapidly gaining force, and no one knows when it will crest.

The author covered the casino industry for the Philadelphia Inquirer in 1988-92 and is now, as David Cay Johnston, a reporter for the *New York Times*.

Gambling and Politics

Between January 1993 and October 1995, gaming interests were big contributors to politicians. Computer analysis and reporting show:

- Gambling political action committees and industry leaders contributed $3.1 million to political parties and candidates.
- $2 million went to Republicans, $1.1 million to Democrats.
- Republican Bob Dole netted $345,850 at a June fund-raiser arranged by Mirage Resorts Inc. Chairman Steve Wynn.
- Republican Lamar Alexander has netted $34,250 during his presidential bid.
- In California, the gaming lobby has spent over $10 million since 1990 as the state mulled initiatives.

Top Gambling Givers

1. Mashantucket Pequot tribe	$465,000
2. Harrah's Entertainment	$380,931
3. Mirage Resorts	$350,000
4. Station Casinos	$324,025
5. Bally's Grand	$232,175
6. Circus Circus	$157,515
7. GTECH	$114,774
8. Boyd Gaming	$89,000

Top Senate Recipients

1. Richard Bryan (D-NV)	$122,180
2. Harry Reid (D-NV)	$30,500
3. Alan Wheat (D-MO) defeated	$25,500
4. Frank Lautenberg (D-NJ)	$25,000
5. Hal Furman (R-NV) defeated	$22,750
6. Chuck Haytalan (R-NJ)defeated	$22,100
7. Fred Thompson (R-TN)	$20,250
8. Edward Kennedy (D-MA)	$16,500

Top House Recipients

1. John Ensign (R-NV)	$143,325
2. Barbara Vucanovich (R-NV)	$46,350
3. James Bilbray (D-NV) defeated	$44,466
4. William Gormley (R-NJ) defeated	$28,300
5. Frank LoBlondo (R-NJ)	$16,500
6. Richard Gephardt (D-MO)	$12,000
7. Patrick Kennedy (D-RI)	$9,750
8. Rod DeBerry (R-TN)defeated	$6,300

USN&WR January 15, 1996
Basic data: Federal Election Commission, Common Cause

Part II
States Roll the Dice
Betting on the Economy

As factories close and federal dollars for states dry up, politicians are increasingly turning to casinos as a way of boosting ailing local economies. As Marc Cooper points out in the following article from the *Nation*, "America's House of Cards," it's no coincidence that they pop up in some of the poorest areas of the country, locales most willing to make the gamble. "To look at the clumps of casinos now clogging the heartland is to look at a map of every place that once had a booming industry—or had none at all. Like a toadstool blooming on rotted wood, a casino will be replacing the steel industry in Gary, Indiana, America's murder capital in 1993."

Las Vegas being one notable exception, casinos rarely do much good for the communities that host them. Despite the promise of jobs and economic renewal, small retailers and restaurants are often driven out of business. A one-room diner simply can't compete with an outrageously cheap casino restaurant; clothing and music stores lose dollars to one-armed bandits. "Because casinos have artificially high profit margins, are often owned by out-of-area investors, and frequently take dollars from the area's existing tourist base rather than attracting new tourists," wrote University of Illinois economist Earl Grinols in the spring 1995 *Illinois Business Review*, "the effect of gambling in many cases is to diminish the economic base and cost jobs." Clearly, gambling is at best a short-term solution, diverting resources from wiser, more reliable development plans.

America's House of Cards

How the Casino Economy Robs the Working Poor

Marc Cooper

The Nation, February 19, 1996

Davenport, Iowa. "I'm a man on a mission, a man committed to all-out war," the Rev. Tom Grey tells me as we stand on the hill overlooking his Mississippi River town of Galena, Illinois. Grey may be a Methodist minister, but it's his experience as a Vietnam infantry vet and his ongoing work as a lieutenant colonel in the Army Reserve that shape his speech. "This time around we're the ones who have the guerrillas among the people, we're the ones winning the hearts and minds. The enemy is being surrounded."

The enemy, "the predator" that Grey wants to "hunt down and destroy," is the burgeoning national gambling industry. And Grey's adversaries are just as visible as the behemoth U.S. choppers that rattled over the Indochinese jungle like giant floating targets. Whereas just ten years ago casino gambling was found only in Nevada and Atlantic City, Americans now lose some $40 billion a year in hundreds of casinos spread over twenty-seven states. Gambling is the new American pastime. Seventy million go to pro baseball games each year; 125 million visit casinos.

"I'm not a prohibitionist," says Grey, field coordinator of the National Coalition Against Legalized Gambling. "This isn't an issue of personal morality. This is about social morality, about an issue of social justice, a battle for who we are in America." Growing more angry as he speaks, he adds, "And this is about pure greed. Either we decide as a country to build a future on solid economic foundations that mean something for our kids and our grandchildren, or we build a casino economy where we say it doesn't matter, America isn't gonna be here so go try and hit a jackpot; a casino economy where you have a mass sellout, where you empty out the middle, making the rich richer and the poor poorer. Let's call gambling what it is, not pass it off as economic development."

Grey's grass-roots organizing efforts have halted the building of any new American casino since 1994. So successful has his counterinsurgency been—defeating pro-gambling referendums about 90 percent of the time in twenty-three contests—that one top gambling consultant has likened the 55-year-old minister to Adolf Hitler. But Grey draws from a long past of liberal social activism, pastoring an inner-city congregation, protesting the invasions of Grenada and Panama, even publicly questioning the Gulf War while in the active Army Reserve. And while he uses the left's language to decry gambling—denouncing the "greedy wedding of bottom-line entrepreneurs and cynical politicians who have given up on America"—most of his volunteer foot soldiers are from the right.

Grey's tactical alliances include the Christian Coalition and the fundamentalist Traditional Values Coalition. Except for some antigambling statements from California State Senator Tom Hayden and U.S. Representative John Conyers, Grey doesn't hear as much as boo from progressives. "This is a natural issue for the left, but it is nowhere to be found," Grey tells me. "When I went up before Congress to testify, Barney Frank told me gambling was an issue of personal choice. Well, Barney Frank just doesn't get it. And frankly, I don't get how in hell the left is so slow to come around to this issue."

Grey's befuddlement is legitimate. Gambling in today's United States—repackaged, sanitized, video-ized, down-marketed and ubiquitous—is not an issue of temperance or free choice but rather one of social class and public economic policy. Here we have an industry popping up in areas devastated by Reaganomics (under any of its names) and imposing the most regressive of taxes on the most vulnerable part of the population, while simultaneously sucking away millions of dollars from

whatever is left of the rest of local economies. But in this election year, in this uncertain economic climate, the issue has so
far been ceded—by default—to pseudo-moralists like Richard
Lugar, Pat Buchanan and the Christian Coalition's Ralph Reed,
who have been the only major political voices to speak out
against the proliferation of legalized gambling.

You could have gone to the G.O.P. presidential debate in
Des Moines last month, as I did, and strained to hear some allu-
sion to the plight of working Iowans as they struggle with
poverty-level wages. The only candidate who even mentioned
creating something as grudging as $10-an-hour manufacturing
jobs was businessman Morry Taylor, who, upon acquiring a
wheel company, stripped his workers of their pensions and
retirement health benefits. Or you could, like the rest of the
chattering classes, obsessively speculate on the emergence of
Steve Forbes as Bob Dole's leading challenger. While the pun-
dits spill tons of ink over the implausible prospect that Forbes's
flat tax might ever be enacted, much more about the future of
ordinary Americans can be learned by looking at the riverboat
gambling casinos twinkling just a few yards outside the Iowa
hotel rooms of the traveling White House press corps. For if
Lenin once summed up Communism as "Soviet power plus
electrification," the highest formulaic expression of the New
American Economy might just be "casinos plus part-time jobs."

Quad Cities meet where Davenport and Bettendorf,
Iowa, shake hands with Moline and Rock Island, Illinois,
across the muddy Mississippi. It's no accident that this is
where America's gambling fever has incubated and spread
over the past half-decade. To look at the clumps of casinos
now clogging the heartland is to look at a map of every place
that once had a booming industry—or had none at all. Like a
toadstool blooming on rotted wood, a casino will be replacing
the steel industry in Gary, Indiana, American's murder capital
in 1993. The most lucrative of Illinois's nine riverboats,
Harrah's, rakes in a royal take of $210 million a year from its
berth in Joliet, where it has replaced the Caterpillar tractor
plant as the town's biggest employer. East St. Louis, described

by the *St. Louis Post-Dispatch* as "America's Soweto," with no obstetric services, no regular trash collection and 75 percent of its almost all-black population on welfare, is now saddled with casino gambling. Other boats jostle for space downriver in poverty-stricken Tunica, Mississippi, traditionally known as the "Ethiopia of America."

And here in the Quad Cities, three riverboats now compete within a five-minute drive of one another, two on the Iowa side of the river, one on the Illinois side. Such a concentration is a sad spectacle in this area, once known as the "Detroit of the farm belt" for its headquartering of mighty John Deere and International Harvester, which produced the heavy machinery that plowed and harvested the fields of the world. I.H. cranked out fleets of the legendary Big Red tractors, which became an icon of rural and prosperous America. Nearby Alcoa ran the biggest aluminum-rolling mill in the world. "Those industrial jobs were so good that I remember back in the sixties college kids buying overalls and working in those factories at night knowing they'd make more money that way than when after they'd graduate," says local historian Ronald Tweet.

If downtown Davenport and Rock Island look postnuclear now, you can date the holocaust to the early eighties. "The reason we have these riverboats today is because of the economic crisis of the last decade," says Tom Fennelly, who as director of Davenport's Eastern Iowa Center for Problem Gambling has seen his client list "jump tenfold" since the local boats opened in 1991. "Case tractors left, I.H. closed down, Cat left, Deere laid off thousands. It was literally 'last man leaving please turn out the lights.'" The farm crisis, the Reagan recession of 1981-82, the overall shifts in the economy and the disastrous results of a couple of marathon strikes against intractable managements hit this area like the apocalypse.

By the end of 1984, 35,000 jobs in a metropolitan community of 400,000 had been cut. Unemployment, fluttering between 17 percent and 22 percent, was the highest in the country after Flint, Michigan. Between 1980 and 1985, Iowa lost a higher percentage of its population to internal migration than any other state in the Union. Eight million square feet of industrial floor space lay empty. "We waited and waited for two, three, four years for someone, anyone, to come in and take up the slack, something like maybe a Saturn plant," says Professor Tweet. "Who would have guessed it would have been riverboats?"

In 1989, two Iowa state legislators—both Democrats, by the way—took on the formidable task of convincing this puritanical state, one that owned all liquor stores and was known to raid church bingo games, to lay its chips on the table. This followed five years of dogged lobbying by the gambling industry, which had been looking precisely for some busted-out place like Davenport as a site to break the national tradition of casino bans.

The political strategy they used promised kinder, gentler gaming—not wicked gambling. Promotional materials pictured a neat fleet of noble paddle-wheelers steaming on the Mississippi while curious out-of-towners sipped wine, munched Brie and, oh yes, laid a few bucks down on the green felt. The gambling stakes would be kept small, to attract wholesome families and not urban gambling junkies. Gaming would take place only during limited two-hour cruises. Maximum bets would be $5. A limit of a $200 loss per day would be imposed. "It's a fool's game. It's entertainment-style gaming," said one of the two sponsors of the measure at the time. "We're selling the lore of Mark Twain," said Robert Arnould, then Democratic majority leader of the Iowa House. Opposition to the gambling proposal was countered with assurances that a healthy portion of casino revenues would be gathered up in new taxes and that another portion would be earmarked for social improvement projects.

This political soft-shoe turned the trick. Even organized labor signed on, knowing full well that the new casino jobs would be nonunion. "We were deeply involved in and strongly supported bringing in the riverboats," says Jerry Messer, president of the Quad City Labor Federation. "You know, the lesser of two evils. Either work on a boat or be unemployed. I believe in everybody making a paycheck."

After a popular referendum to seal the deal, the first of the new generation of riverboat casinos—the *Diamond Lady* docked in Bettendorf and the *President* in Davenport—opened their tables and slots on April 1, 1991. Disneyland's *Columbia* is much closer to a real paddle-wheeler, the new casinos being little more than glorified barges with a thin film of Mississippi riverboat gloss. But that was of little concern to the endless caravan of buses from wealthy Chicago and the surrounding states that brought in hundreds of thousands of gamblers for one-day turnarounds. Indeed, in the year the *President* opened, a full 40 percent of its patrons came from Chicago ZIP codes.

A panic immediately gripped the neighboring states. Soon, Mississippi legalized its own casinos and—unlike Iowa—did away with all pretenses, allowing patrons to lose as much as they liked and, in addition, not actually have to go out and cruise the river. Illinois followed suit, eliminating the $200 loss limit while maintaining the cruise requirement. The prairie wildfire had been touched off, and casino lights began to blaze from impoverished ports and Indian reservations throughout the heartland.

The competition devastated Iowa's boats (their owners, in the meantime, had built exactly *none* of the land-based tourist developments they'd promised in the lobbying campaign). Within two years, out-of-town visits fell to less than 15 percent of casino business. The *Diamond Lady* in Bettendorf lifted anchor and floated down to the more liberal no-cruise/no-limit state of Mississippi; the *Emerald Lady* in Fort Madison, Iowa, also weighed anchor for Mississippi. These departures dumped 600 workers out of their jobs and left the town holding the bag for a $2.6 million tax-dollar investment in a municipal dock.

"'Chasin' the losses' is what we call it when compulsive gamblers up the stakes trying to recoup previous losses," says treatment counselor Fennelly. "When the other states took away part of the casino traffic, Iowa, by now itself an addict, started chasin' its losses." In fact, as competition among the river states surpassed any back-alley cutthroat game of Texas Hold 'Em, Iowa threw Tom and Huck overboard and went instead for the Meyer Lansky approach.

By 1994, Iowa was dependent on gambling revenue and answerable to a new constituency of riverboat owners, workers and gambling addicts. Responding to a vigorous lobbying campaign led by a prominent G.O.P. lawyer, the state dropped its quaint $200 loss limit, loosened the requirement that casinos actually cruise the river and went for full-bore, round-the-clock dockside gambling. To fight off the out-of-state competition, Iowa also *reduced* gambling taxes, expanded off-track betting and actually took over ownership of a collapsing racetrack in Des Moines, turning it profitable by legalizing the installation of hundreds of slot machines. The state had moved from regulator to pit boss. "With each liberalization, from the allowing of more A.T.M.s to the lifting of limits, to the end of cruising requirements, our client base would incrementally jump," says Fennelly.

No matter that each compulsive gambler costs the taxpayers between $13,000 and $35,000 a year in treatment, law enforcement, divorce, spousal battering and absenteeism. No matter that Iowa's compulsive-gambling population has more than tripled since the boats opened, from 1.7 percent to 5.4 percent. "Before the boats came I used to gamble a maximum of once a year in Las Vegas and limit myself to maybe a $500 loss," says Linda Edwards, a 45-year-old single mother who drives a forklift for John Deere. "When the *President* opened in 1991 it was like a new adventure. I went the second night it opened and I lost the $200 limit." Soon Edwards was back, at first once a month or so, then once a week, then every night. As the limits were lifted, she fell deeper into debt. "I'd play one slot machine at a time, mostly quarter slots. At first I could go through the $200 limit in fifteen minutes. When the limit was lifted I could stay all night." Eventually she was maxing out credit cards, taking out personal loans, even bouncing checks in the casino itself. Last year, when she was $75,000 in the hole and thinking of suicide, she sought treatment. "I came on the boats to escape my problems. I was already behind in my bills, [had] problems with my boyfriend and my daughter, so what the heck? It was the excitement. There's not much to do around here, and the boat was like a candy store."

The Saturday afternoon of the Iowa presidential debate the pit manager of Davenport's *President* swears casino attendance is abnormally high. "Maybe that debate brought more people in," he laughs as he signs a credit voucher for one bearded gambler in a Harley T-shirt. Any daily attendance bump would be hard to figure, as casino patronage in Iowa has been climbing astronomically since the liberalization of 1994—up nearly 100 percent in 1994 to 3.1 million visits. The state now has nine riverboats.

The *President* is the largest of them, but on this day there is standing room only at the crap, roulette and 21 tables. (In part because there are proportionally fewer gaming tables than in Vegas, the riverboats' more downscale clientele favor the slots and video poker machines.) The dress is strictly jeans, workboots, flannel shirts and baseball caps. The gnarled hands of workers and farmers snap up cards dealt from across the table by the equally gnarled hands of former factory workers now making the average $19,000 a year paid to those 60 percent of casino employees who are full time—or by recent high school graduates whose career aspiration is to graduate to Reno or Las Vegas.

These floating casinos are what Professor Robert Goodman calls "convenience gambling" in his just-published book, *The Luck Business*. The 7-Elevens of the industry, they are to the Vegas mega-casinos what crack cocaine is to pure Colombian snow. This is like the town carnival that never closes and never leaves. Always open to empty your pockets, the casinos endlessly recycle desperate and now mostly local day-trippers. One doesn't have to stay long at any table to see the visible pain that comes with the loss of a $5 or $10 bet, the high number of "players" digging deep into their purses or pockets for that ciggy money they'll put down to chase the loss.

Statistics show that the poor are likely to spend two-and-a-half times the percentage of their income on gambling as the middle class. And with the stock market and limited-part-nership opportunities not much of a draw among K Mart workers, gambling is the only "investment" many of the working poor think they can afford. A full 27 percent of lower-income gamblers polled in one study said they were in the casino "to get rich." Yet the average result of each gambling visit is a loss of between $25 and $100.

Of the total casino take, a city like Davenport gets about $1 per gambler head in tax revenue. A similar amount—more than $2 million a year—flows into a local development fund that is then doled out in dozens of grants to schools, police forces, homeless shelters, charities and so on. In Davenport in 1992 the biggest grant—$750,000—went directly to the business elite in the form of an expansion of the city's convention center. Another 15 percent of the take goes to the state. The other 80 percent of the casino revenue, hundreds of millions of dollars, is transferred from the pockets of the gamblers into the pockets of the owners—some local, some based in Las Vegas.

It's a chilling experience to stand in front of any one of these riverboat casinos and realize that each year a million or more people flock to it and yet there is, apart from parking lots, nothing, absolutely nothing—not a bar, a cafe, a hamburger shop, a souvenir stand—that has sprung up near it. Gamblers want to gamble, not shop. And no restaurant can compete with the casinos' $6 all-you-can-eat buffets of prime rib and seafood. Those few who still come on buses from out of town apparently see no reason to stay overnight in the Quad Cities.

The casinos produce no wealth (except for the owners, of course). No goods are manufactured or exchanged. Almost every dollar lost in the casino is "cannibalized," sucked out of the community and not spent somewhere else or, God forbid, socked away in a savings account. Last year in Iowa and Illinois alone more than $4 billion was lost on one form or another of legal gambling. That's about *three times* the revenue earned from gambling by cities and states in the entire rest of the country. A just-completed review by *U.S. News & World Report* of fifty-five counties that got casinos between 1990 and 1992 shows they had no more growth than similar counties without casinos, and in some cases they lost local businesses.

"Since the boats have come in, all we see is more people needing help of more kinds," says Chuck Landon of Churches United of the Quad Cities Area. "And things are supposed to be getting better! The gambling appeals to the very people who can least afford it." I talk with Landon in the Martin Luther King Community Center, which is surrounded on four sides by sprawling empty lots. On those fields used to prosper the commercial heart of Rock Island's black community. Now little business is left even in the white-dominated downtown. Landon helps coordinate a network of church-run food pantries that serve more than 30,000 people a year in the Quad Cities. But surely, I ask him, you can't blame all that need on just the introduction of casinos?

"Of course not," he answers. "Let me say we do see a lot of people gambling their food money away. But we served food to 11,000 families last year. That's one out of ten in the Quad Cities. That's families, not homeless or vagrants. These are largely unemployed or, more likely, underemployed. Despite the official version that we are in a period of rebuilding, more and more people just aren't making it. A state study shows that by the year 2000, 70 percent of jobs in this area will pay less than $20,000 a year. That's the problem." Indeed, unemployment levels hover at a reasonable 5 percent, but Quad Cities wages run 10 percent or more below the national average.

Later that afternoon, a few blocks away, Vince Thomas, who runs Project NOW, one of Rock Island's largest nonprofit social service agencies, pulls out a file of state reports and statistics. One set of numbers tells it all: Though the overall population has decreased, there were nearly twice as many residents of Rock Island County on food stamps and/or public assistance in March 1995—a time of "recovery" with roughly 5 percent unemployment—than there were in the summer of 1982, when the local economy was flattening out and joblessness was in the high double digits. "If you had kidnaped me in 1982 when the economy collapsed, held me incommunicado on Mars and dropped me back here last week, I would tell you that nothing has changed," says Thomas. "The only difference is, where we once served the unemployed, we increasingly serve more of the working poor who need help with clothing, energy bills, food bills and, most of all, rent and housing assistance." Five years after the panacea of legalized gambling, 47 percent of Rock Island County residents are classified as "low, very low or extremely low income," though 95 percent of them are employed.

And starting this year, Rock Islanders are being saddled with the extra burden of *directly* subsidizing their one casino riverboat. Squeezed by Iowa's more liberal dockside, no-cruise gambling, the Rock Island Casino has seen its receipts plummet; even so, 14 percent of the city's operating funds derived from casino revenues as late as 1994. Rock Island has had to factor out that income from its budget for this coming fiscal year, so jobs have been cut and taxes have been raised to make up the shortfall. And now the city is rebating all casino taxes owed it if the riverboat's revenue is less than its monthly cash losses. So far, this city of 40,000 has returned nearly half a million dollars in tax money to the casino owners. "We can't get the city to give us a $15,000 grant for minority businesses and a job search program," says John Carroll of the Alliance for Justice. "But it gives hundreds of thousands of dollars in tax abatements to the riverboats and then raises our water bills to pay for it."

The most jarring thing about the Quad Cities is the fact that their overall economic situation is now considered absolutely normal in America's new postindustrial era. Except for a handful of activists like Landon and Thomas, no one in the establishment dares speak of crisis. All you hear about is the low unemployment rate.

"Our economy is very, very rosy. Robust and diversified," says Larry Reed of Davenport's Chamber of Commerce. "The local economy is healthy and growing," concurs Republican Mayor Patrick Gibbs, sitting beneath a signed photo of Newt Gingrich. The riverboats, he says, are economic development.

As proof of revival, he points to the arrival of a telemarketing firm providing a few hundred jobs at $16,000 a year. When I ask what sort of business boom the boats have brought, the Mayor boasts of a downtown Starbucks-like coffee bar, one that seats maybe six or eight people and certainly employs fewer.

These two officials are no different from thousands of others across the country, at both the local and national levels. The scene in Davenport is repeated in hundreds of other American communities. Local industry collapses in the global market. Local commerce goes with it, leaving downtown boarded up and joblessness in the stratosphere. Service industries move in to exploit the battered work force and national retail chains open up on the fringe strip malls, driving the final stake into Main Street, while local banks and TV stations are snapped up by out-of-town networks. Jobs reappear—albeit at subsistence wages. Victory is declared. The only problem for local officials is finding an adequate tax base. Along the Mississippi River that dilemma has been solved by the riverboats. Now the poor can throw their money on the table—and get new convention centers in return.

The day I receive Larry Reed's "rosy" economic forecast there's a near-riot at the Moline Holiday Inn. America's twenty-ninth Farm and Fleet store—a retail outlet like K Mart or Sears—is soon to open out on John Deere Road. A ten-day "Job Fair" has been scheduled at the hotel to fill the 200 open positions—40 percent of them part time, average starting wage less than $6 an hour. A thousand applications have been printed for the week-and-a-half event. But within the first five hours they are gone and the swelling throng of job seekers, packed elbow to elbow in the Holiday Inn banquet room, is angry. "My God, to see this kind of turnout for something like this, it's sad," says 41-year-old Betty VanEckhouette, out of a full-time job for the past four years. "They're scraping to get these $6-an-hour jobs. How can you sustain a family on $6 an hour?"

With new casino construction stalled by growing local backlashes, the next battle over gambling will take place at the national level. Partisans on both sides are readying to fight over a measure proposed by Senator Paul Simon and Representative John Conyers that would create a national commission to study the effects of widespread gambling.

The commission bill will most likely be approved. But any proposed rollback or ban on gambling will meet a wall of resistance from the industry lobby, which is aggressively buying its political standing [see "Vegas Bob," February 12]. Meanwhile the industry's full-time foe, Tom Grey, hopes that before this political season is over, legalized gambling will surface in the national debate. "What an opportunity for us," says Grey of the '96 campaign. "Where else in America could we catch all the bad guys together at the feeding trough? We could really clean house. The right, the left, all of American has to come together and ask what we want as an economic foundation for the next century." And Grey continues to believe his eventual success depends on bringing the left on board. "Liberals tend to look at 'isms.' They don't see the little battles that open the door to the big battles," he laments. "The left keeps closing the door, withdrawing, giving up on the people in the middle. They'd rather attack the right than talk to ordinary folks in between. Unfortunately for the left, it's the right which is doing a much better job of talking to the middle."

While Grey is waiting for the left to come around, the gambling industry is forging ahead with plans for expansion. At a recent gambling industry summit in Las Vegas, Melvin Simon, whose company helped build the mammoth Mall of America in Bloomington, Minnesota, said he envisions the day when casinos, not department stores, will be the anchor of the country's malls. "It will take a lot of legislation," said Simon. "But believe me, it's a possibility."

Casinos
Not a Sure Bet,
Other States Discover

Analysts Say Area Officials Could Learn
From Successes and Failures Elsewhere

Charles Babington

Washington Post, August 6, 1995

Anchored on the Mississippi River near downtown New Orleans are two massive, double-decker casino boats with the evocative names *Crescent City Queen* and *Grand Palais*.

There's nothing grand about them now, however. Both boats closed their doors last month, barely nine weeks after opening amid much hoopla and hope. The closings, forced by lower-than-expected revenue, left 1,800 people jobless and the City of New Orleans jockeying with other creditors to collect $3 million in unpaid taxes and fees.

The turn of events has been sobering—even on Bourbon Street—and may give pause to officials in Maryland, Virginia, the District and elsewhere who are contemplating legalizing casinos. Although some southern and midwestern towns are content with their riverboat revenue, others are finding that the reality does not always match the promise.

That's especially true in New Orleans, a city that bears watching by the likes of Baltimore and Washington, according to several analysts. Aside from the loss of the two riverboat casinos, New Orleans' ambitious land-based casino has netted only a third of its projected revenue since opening in May.

The picture is brighter in the Midwest. One reason, however, is that lawmakers quickly relaxed regulations that had made casinos politically palatable in the first place. In Davenport, Iowa, a riverboat casino netted $14 million last year after legislators increased its operating hours and dropped a rule that had limited each gambler's loss to $200 a visit.

Those changes lured thousands of gamblers from a nearby casino boat in Rock Island, Ill. As a result, more than 200 people lost jobs there, and Rock Island now receives only a fraction of the $4 million in casino tax revenue that it got two years ago.

In Missouri, six riverboat casinos poured $79 million into state and local tax coffers last year. Again, looser regulations helped. Slot machines—initially banned in Missouri—were added to the table games.

A political cloud is looming, however. Missouri's attorney general alleges that the state House speaker broke the law by accepting thousands of dollars from casino companies and trying to influence licensing decisions. A grand jury is investigating.

Against this national backdrop, Maryland is preparing for a legislative decision on casinos this winter, a D.C. group has asked the elections board to place a casino initiative on the District's 1996 ballot, and an industry-backed coalition is still pushing for riverboat casinos in Virginia after three consecutive legislative setbacks.

Industry analysts conclude that under the right circumstances, casinos can boost local economies and government coffers, sometimes dramatically. But they say casinos are not a panacea for politicians hoping to revitalize a failing city or finance a state government while cutting taxes.

"Although casinos are spreading to more states, they have limited potential as a source of tax revenue," said Steven D. Gold, director of the Center for the Study of the States, in Albany, N.Y. Casinos take some money that otherwise would be spent on state lotteries or taxable goods and services, he said. Moreover, the growing number of casinos nationwide will result in smaller potential for new ones.

"There will never be another Nevada," Gold wrote recently. Nor, experts say, will there be another Atlantic City, where a dozen large casinos attract busloads of bettors to an otherwise blighted town.

Since 1990, six midwestern and southern states have legalized commercial, non-Indian casinos. (Federally recognized Indian tribes can operate casinos without state approval or tax assessments, and the casinos are highly successful in Connecticut and elsewhere.)

The six states are the guinea pigs now being scrutinized by cities and states trying to decide whether casinos are a good public bet. Among the groups conducting inquiries are a government-appointed task force in Maryland and the Greater Washington Board of Trade. Casino companies are keen on the Washington area because it would help them crack the untapped mid-Atlantic region.

In Maryland, proposals range from a few small casinos, possibly at horse-racing tracks or in mountain counties, to large betting palaces in downtown Baltimore and the PortAmerica site in Prince George's County, near the Woodrow Wilson Bridge. If Baltimore and the D.C. suburbs are the ultimate targets, several analysts say, then New Orleans might be the most analogous site for scrutiny. Like Baltimore and the District, it is a city with a well-established tourist trade but serious problems of crime and middle-class flight.

In 1991 and 1992, when Louisiana legislators approved 15 floating casinos throughout the state and one large land-based casino in New Orleans, boosters said gambling would be a surefire winner. In the last four months, however, three of New Orleans's five floating casinos have closed, eliminating the jobs of hundreds of people who thought the boats would bring them a better life. Meanwhile, Harrah's temporary land-based casino has earned about $12 million a month, far short of the $33 million that was projected. The company is building a mammoth, permanent casino that officials hope will draw more gamblers when it opens next summer in the heart of the touristy French Quarter.

Some critics say the setbacks are the inevitable result of Louisiana's greed and haste in approving casinos, a process that enriched several friends of the high-stakes gambling governor, Edwin Edwards. "It's the same scam going on worldwide," said New Orleans lawyer C.B. Forgotson Jr.

Forgotson said casino companies promise the moon without conducting realistic studies of who will come to gamble. Eventually, he said, "they find out the only people coming to casinos are locals. So then you are cannibalizing your local business...The same thing is going to happen in Detroit and Baltimore."

Other analysts, however, say New Orleans is temporarily suffering from foolish decisions that other states can avoid.

"The root of the problem is that the wrong people were licensed, and they were licensed for political reasons," said Larry Pearson, publisher of the New Orleans-based Riverboat Gaming Report. He noted that riverboat casinos in other parts of Louisiana are doing well.

Only a few states have been willing to try a non-Indian, land-based casino. In Mississippi and the four Midwestern states with casinos, the facilities must be on boats, even though some never leave the dock.

Many analysts say "riverboat gambling" is a political ploy to ease the worries of some voters who associate land-based casinos with Las Vegas's tackiness and Atlantic City's grit. "State legislators think that a little cruise with a paddle wheel somehow makes it not gambling," said Brian Ford, a Philadelphia-based casinos adviser for the accounting firm Ernst & Young.

Some analysts argue that if Washington and Baltimore want casinos, they should build big Vegas-like facilities that could lure tourists and large conventions.

"Scattering some riverboats around the Washington-Baltimore area would be a disaster," said Hunter Barrier, director of the Alexandria-based Gaming and Economic Development Institute. Most tourists would ignore such facilities, he said, "So revenues will come from local residents. And that money would come from restaurants, theaters and other local businesses."

It is just that scenario that has prompted Maryland's restaurant and thoroughbred racing industries to unite against casinos. They say casinos typically supply bettors with cheap food and a fast-paced array of slot machines and card games that make horse races seem poky.

"Casinos would have a devastating impact on our industry," said Marcia Harris, of the Restaurant Association of Maryland.

Despite opposition to casinos from racing and restaurant interests, politicians in Maryland and elsewhere are tempted for a simple reason. Tax rates on casino earnings are typically about 20 percent, four times the level of Maryland's 5 percent sales tax. If a resident spends $100 in a casino rather than in a clothing store, the store suffers, but the state receives $20 rather than $5.

Barrier said most governments that are contemplating casinos focus on three concerns: crime, compulsive gambling and "product substitution," or the losses to non-casino businesses when their customers gamble.

"I've come to the conclusion that crime is not a problem," Barrier said, an opinion supported by several studies and interviews with police officials in towns with riverboat casinos. But problem gambling, he said, is "something that has to be looked at real carefully."

Problem gambling is hard to measure, authorities say, and casino supporters note that most Americans already have ample opportunities to bet on lotteries and other ventures. However, a 1994 study of legalized gambling, funded by the Aspen Institute, a D.C. think tank, and the Ford Foundation, concluded: "There is a direct increase in the numbers of people with pathological gambling problems as a result of increases in legalization."

As for product substitution, a debate rages. Casino supporters say everyone in a community benefits if casinos hire new workers, attract tourist dollars and contribute to higher tax revenue.

There's not much hard data on the subject. In South Dakota, where Indian casinos operate, a 1991 state study found no appreciable drop in overall taxable retail sales. However, there were "significant declines for selected activities such as clothing stores, recreation services, business services, auto dealers and service stations."

When casinos open, "existing vendors lose," said Jeff Finkle, executive director of the Washington-based National Council of Urban Economic Development. Nonetheless, he predicts that Maryland and Virginia officials will find it hard to withstand the lure of casino revenue, especially if Pennsylvania, West Virginia or Delaware threaten to strike first.

"Somebody in this area is going to do it," Finkle told a Greater Washington Board of Trade task force last week. "It is inevitable, and when it happens it will hurt D.C." unless a revenue-sharing agreement is reached.

Rural Renewal

But Poverty Persists
as Casinos Thrive in Mississippi County

Stephanie Saul
December 10, 1995
Newsday, Inc. Copyright © 1995
From the Series "Gambling: The New National Pastime"

Tunica County, Miss.—All that Lynn Neas has to do to explain the death of her restaurant is to point toward the Mississippi River levee, where seven garish casinos loom incongruously over the surrounding cotton fields.

The Hollywood bar and restaurant she managed in a 135-year-old plantation commissary closed this year, a victim of the gambling fever that has taken hold in this Old South state.

Known for its soulful blues musicians and authentic fried catfish, the Hollywood, in Robinsonville, was one of the few reasons outsiders ever came to Tunica County, a sleepy, dusty farming hamlet 30 miles south of Memphis.

Now, thousands visit here each day, but most of them eat free buffets given away by the casinos to lure customers.

"It's hard for a restaurant to compete with what they have in prices," said Neas, who hopes to reopen someday. "We can't offer free food."

Once the poorest county in the poorest state in the nation, Tunica's economy has changed practically overnight with the birth of a prosperous casino gambling industry here. Since October, 1992, when the first casino opened, the county's budget has swelled from $3 million to $25 million a year. The gaming industry points to Tunica as its newest success story, a modern-day gambling mecca rising from the cotton fields just as Las Vegas rose up out of the desert 50 years ago.

"We're trying to become a destination," said Webster Franklin, a former aide to Vice President Dan Quayle who now runs the Tunica Chamber of Commerce. Franklin envisions golf courses, theme parks, shopping centers. Already, several motels have opened to house gamblers.

But, even here, casino gambling is not without its drawbacks, as Neas' story illustrates. Some local businesses are strained by competition from casinos, and the 8,000 new casino jobs haven't gone to Tunica's poorest residents, many of whom still live in sharecropper shacks. Crime has increased by 800 percent, according to District Attorney Laurence Mellen.

"There's a trade-off and the glitter costs," said Mellen. "It costs in the way of crime and in fear."

Once viewed as the breath of life for dying cities, the elixir for decaying tourist destinations, casino gambling in some form has been approved in 25 states. Nationally, casinos got 125 million visits last year, making gambling America's fastest-growing industry.

But casino gambling has not delivered everything its backers predicted. And the nation is undergoing a collective reality check, of sorts, on the benefits of casino gambling, even as New York, which currently allows only one Indian-run casino near Utica, moves closer to approving commercial casinos. The legislature approved the development of casinos in Buffalo, Niagara Falls, the Adirondacks and the Catskills last year. Another legislative vote is required, as well as a statewide referendum, before the casinos get final approval.

In Illinois, a study last month concluded that riverboat casinos had not spurred development in five cities, as their supporters had predicted.

"It is clear that our study shows there has been no economic development and no tourism," the Chicago Better Government Association, a public interest group, concluded in a report. The casinos raised tax revenues for the state, but created no jobs in surrounding communities, the study found. "Casino gambling does not create jobs. It creates nothing of value. There is no economic development and the study shows that riverboat gambling in Illinois fails any test for tourism," the association said.

With financial support from the casino industry, New Orleans officials have begun a $1.2 million study of the effects of casino gambling after the failures of two of four riverboat casinos. Harrah's, in the process of constructing one of the world's largest land-based casinos on Canal Street, halted construction, closed its temporary location and laid off 2,500 workers last month. Lenders for the project bailed out after low earnings projections.

A Maryland task force on casino gambling visited riverboats in St. Louis and casinos in Atlantic City before voting "no" last month. A dearth of information made it impossible to calculate the benefits of allowing casino gambling in Maryland, the task force concluded. Projections had varied widely. One state study estimated there would be a net loss of 19,000 jobs if Maryland legalized casino gambling. But another study by a consulting firm and the University of Baltimore estimated a gain of 63,000 jobs.

William Eadington, a University of Nevada expert on gambling issues, told a congressional panel last month: "It is surprising how little is definitively known about the social and economic impacts of this $40 billion a year industry."

John Warren Kindt, an economics professor at the University of Illinois who has conducted several studies of gambling's social cost, estimates that for every dollar gambling generates in tax revenues for a state, the social problems it causes—including theft, embezzlement, insurance fraud and incarceration—cost the state three dollars.

"There's a myth that gambling is a harmless form of entertainment," Kindt said. "But there are very large social costs, which people have forgotten."

Congress is debating whether to form its own commission to study the national gambling phenomenon. Among things it would ponder are Kindt's theory and the extent to which casinos detract from existing local businesses. In his book, *The Luck Business*, Hampshire College professor Robert Goodman calls this later phenomenon cannibalizing. "Instead of bringing new wealth into the community, convenience gambling enterprises cannibalize the local economy."

Cannibalization, however, isn't too much of a problem in places like Tunica County, where retail businesses are few. The Hollywood, which was mentioned in Marc Cohn's 1991 hit song, "Walking in Memphis," was the only retail establishment for miles in the northern part of the county, where the casinos are located. The county of 220,000 acres of cotton and soybean fields hugs the banks of the Mississippi River. Historically, this was a place of sprawling plantations and little else.

With the increasing use of mechanized farm equipment in the middle 20th century, employment here dwindled and many of the area's residents moved north to Memphis or farther north, for jobs in Chicago or Detroit. "This town had been dying," said Franklin. Children who grew up in Tunica County, by and large, left. Many of those who remained collected welfare benefits.

Tunica was so poor that, just 10 years ago, Jesse Jackson called it "America's Ethiopia." And a Tunica neighborhood known euphemistically as "Sugar Ditch Alley," because of an open sewage ditch, became a symbol of poverty in the United States. So when the state of Mississippi approved casino gambling in waterfront counties, Tunica County, with its poverty and proximity to Memphis, seemed a natural location.

The result is practically surreal. Mississippi's casino law says the gaming establishments, called "boats" here, must float. While some lawmakers may have envisioned paddlewheel casinos with Southern charm, the Tunica County casinos are built on barges in dredged canals jutting off the Mississippi River. The river itself is visible only from one casino.

The casinos may as well be built on land. And the architecture is anything but Southern. Fitzgerald's resembles an Irish castle and its visitors are constantly wished "The Luck of the Irish." At Circus, Circus, gambling is under what looks like a big tent. The Hollywood Hotel and Casino features a movie-set theme.

Three casinos have closed or moved to different locations on the river. Those that remain, however, are expanding, adding on theaters, motel rooms, parking lots and, in one case, a golf course. Another casino, Grand's, is scheduled to open next year.

Other development is still in the planning or construction stages. For miles around the remaining casinos, there are no restaurants and only one convenience store and gas station. Roads are being widened as families cluster on collapsing porches, watching quietly as their world changes. As mechanical cotton pickers fill up trailers with the billowing white stuff, signs advertise that fields are available for development.

Entire water, electrical and road systems have been built through cotton fields to accommodate the casinos. At night, streams of traffic wind through the fields on newly-paved roads. A huge influx of gamblers that far outstrips the county's total population comes here daily from Memphis.

Traffic accidents have become routine along the flat roads leading to the casinos. Many occur in the early morning hours, when gamblers, given free drinks at casinos, head back home. The sheriff's department hasn't done a count. But Peggy Cannon, who keeps accident reports for the county, said she formerly used one file folder a year. Now, it's one a month.

Like the gamblers, most of the workers come from Memphis. But welfare rolls have dropped significantly here. In summer 1992, before the casinos came to town, 4,218 of the county's 8,300 people received food stamps. By summer 1995, the food stamp rolls had dropped to 2,780, according to Derrick Crawford, the county's welfare director.

"Casinos are the only thing we can attribute it to," says Crawford.

The casinos have also brought increased crime, according to Mellen, the district attorney. The county averaged about 20 indictments a year before the casinos. That number has gone up to about 160, Mellen said.

"There's an increase in violent crime, armed robberies and sexual crimes," said Mellen. "Knowing the background of the cases, it's because of gambling. They'll lose all their money and steal a car. We had a kidnaping. An older lady was kidnaped and they took her car." Most of the criminals come from out of town, Mellen said.

People who had never gambled before have been enticed by the casinos, according to Delois Bland, a seamstress at Harrah's, who found herself drawn to gamble by an irresistible offer.

The casinos offer to cash paychecks, then give the bearer a free spin on a wheel for a chance to double the paycheck. Advertised heavily on billboards that line U.S. 61, the main highway from Memphis, the "double your paycheck" offer sounds like a winning proposition, because the worker doesn't have to wager anything. To the casinos, it's another way to get potential gamblers in the door. Only the iron-willed can resist the slots and game tables as they exit with a wad of cash.

"If I had my check in my hand, I'd say, 'I'll just stop here,'" Bland said. "Those that can't hold onto it find themselves losing their whole paycheck over there at the casinos, then realizing they could have used the money to pay their light and gas bill."

Bland, an independent dressmaker before the casinos opened, considers herself a beneficiary of the new casino economy. She is now in charge of uniforms at Harrah's. But there are many other longtime residents of Tunica who have been unable to find work in the casino industry, partly due to a high illiteracy rate and partly because of what's locally called the "plantation mentality."

The "plantation mentality" still blocks many of the town's residents, who descended from slaves and sharecroppers, from finding work in the casinos, according to Willie Dismuke Jr., the high school principal. Most of the workers come from Memphis. The local unemployment rate hovers at 14.5 percent.

Unaccustomed to regular schedules, workers have trouble getting to the casinos on time, Dismuke said. "Time doesn't mean very much if you're working on this white man's plantation and you start working when the sun comes up and stop when it goes down," Dismuke explained. Some workers simply stay home when it rains, as they would have in their farm jobs.

The same phenomenon affects schoolwork. "They come to school at 9 o'clock because Mr. John Doe at Plantation A let them come late," Dismuke said.

Test scores at the school rank at the very bottom of the state's 149 public school systems. "They failed the fluency literacy exam," Dismuke says of the students at his school of 547. Dismuke, who once worked as an educator in Chicago, was hired a year ago to improve the academic instruction in the school, which has only nine white students. Most white pupils in the community attend a segregated private academy.

Dismuke placed 250 of the school's pupils in a special tutorial program, and hopes that the results of this year's testing will elevate the school system above level one, the state's lowest designation, and a rating shared by only 11 other schools in the state.

Dismuke says the casinos have helped the schools, both with tax revenues and donations. They catered food for the after-school program, for example.

"A lot of kids are working that never worked before," Dismuke said of the casinos. "A lot of parents are working who haven't worked before."

But Dismuke complains that the bulk of the tax revenues are being used to build roads to "some white man's plantation." Even those who have benefited directly from the casinos complain that the county tax revenues haven't been used to benefit most people

"People in the neighborhoods, we're not seeing it yet," said Bland. "I think they should be putting in better houses and develop more jobs and better recreation."

The county's administrator, Ken Murphree, acknowledged that most of the money is going to shore up the county's infrastructure—paving roads, repairing county buildings and putting an addition onto the jail. "We're not gonna try to give everybody in Tunica County a house," Murphree said. "I'm interested in creating jobs for people so they will be able to provide their own housing."

Down the road, Murphree sees factories and residential development.

But others worry about the future.

Three years after casinos first opened here, there has

already been a shake-out in the Tunica casino industry. Three casinos have closed or moved to different locations on the river, with resulting layoffs. Many workers quit longstanding jobs on farms or in Memphis to join the casinos, only to have them fold.

"Tunica, Mississippi, also happens to be the closest county with riverboat casinos to the Memphis market," said Nelson Rose, a professor at California's Whittier Law School who is an expert on gambling. "How much business would survive if Tennessee legalizes gambling?" Rose notes that the current return on investment for the Tunica casinos is enough that they might not care about the long term.

Victor Toolie, a Tunica construction worker, has reached the same conclusion. "Lady Luck left. The President left," he said, referring to two of the closed casinos. "A lot of the boats make a quick hustle and then they go. Tennessee is going to get boats. A lot of the people who come to the boats are from Tennessee. I'll guess we'll just have to wait and see on down the road."

A Betting Nation†

Twenty-seven states currently have some form of casino gambling, up from two, Nevada and New Jersey, just 10 years ago. Legalized gambling—including lotteries, casinos and parimutuels, such as horse racing—now generates nearly $39.9 billion a year in revenue for states, nonprofits and companies.

What's Being Bet
1994 Gross Wagering by Industry

Parimutuels	$ 17.4 bil.*
Casinos	$367.9 bil.
Indian reservations (all forms of gambling)	$ 41.1 bil.
Lotteries	$ 34.5 bil.

*Includes horse racing, dog racing, jai alai, simulcast and off-track wagering

Where the Wagers are Placed

New casino meccas like Deadwood, S.D., Biloxi, Miss., and Cripple Creek, Colo. have changed the face of an industry once limited to Atlantic City and Las Vegas. That, along with the onslaught of riverboats, card rooms and Indian casino operations, has fueled the industry's $18.8 billion in revenues for 1994.

Sparks, Nev.	17 casinos
Carson City, Nev.	13 casinos
Reno, Nev.	49 casinos
Las Vegas Nev.	206 casinos
Henderson, Nev.	20 casinos
Laughlin, Nev.	10 casinos
Black Hawk, Colo.	19 casinos
Central City, Colo.	12 casinos
Deadwood, S.D.	95 casinos
Cripple Creek, Colo.	21 casinos.
Mashantucket, Conn.	Largest casino in U.S.
Atlantic City, N.J.	12 casinos
Tunica-Robinsonville, Miss.	10 casinos
Biloxi area, Miss.	11 casinos

†Statistics on this and the following pages are from *US News & World Report*, January 15, 1996. See the bottom of page 57 for more information.

Video poker

Thirty-four counties in South Carolina allow video poker machines in locations ranging from taverns to convenience stores. All told, more than 19,000 machines have been licensed.

Card Rooms

Locations ranging from racetracks to bars may offer games such as poker and blackjack; in all, 276 licensed public card rooms exist in Washington State alone, along with 249 in California and 180 in Montana.

A Little Off the Top

Estimated tax revenue for top casino gambling states in 1994

Nevada	$520 mil
New Jersey	*$272 mil
Illinois	$230 mil
Mississippi	$166 mil
Louisiana	$130 mil
Connecticut	**$113 mil
Colorado	$43 mil
Missouri	$30 mil

Note: May not include some state-imposed fees.
*Does not include $42.5 million in taxes paid to the Casino
    Reinvestment Development Authority.
**Figure reflects slot-machine revenue included in unique
    tribal-state compact with Mashantucket Pequots.

The State of Gambling

1994 gross wagering and revenue, in millions

State	Gross wagering*	Gross revenue**
Alabama	$409.0	$87.2
Alaska	$208.5	$46.3
Arizona	$759.2	$225.4
Arkansas	$275.4	$53.0
California	$3,941.0	$2,422.7
Colorado	$5,992.7	$555.8
Connecticut	$1,058.7	$379.1
Delaware	$234.7	$83.9
D.C.	$214.4	$104.3
Florida	$4,212.3	$1,558.0
Georgia	$1,340.8	$591.2

State	Gross wagering*	Gross revenue**
Hawaii	00	
Idaho	$124.2	$42.6
Illinois	$22,377.6	$2,101.7
Indiana	$881.1	$335.3
Iowa	$2,098.8	$245.4
Kansas	$448.7	$136.9
Kentucky	$1,136.7	$388.5
Louisiana	$22,454.5	$1,393.3
Maine	$247.8	$92.3
Maryland	$2,108.7	$717.6
Massachusetts	$3,372.4	$1,110.4
Michigan	$2,022.4	$839.8
Minnesota	$1,610.2	$375.2
Mississippi	$29,874.4	$1,499.4
Missouri	$2,811.6	$335.7
Montana	$2,219.9	$238.1
Nebraska	$598.1	$78.5
Nevada	$210,932.2	$7,071.1
New Hampshire	$426.9	$135.4
New Jersey	$78,717.3	$4,429.6
New Mexico	$207.8	$46.8
New York	$5,781.7	$1,975.6
North Carolina	$34.8	$8.3
North Dakota	$557.9	$66.2
Ohio	$3,199.0	$1,167.1
Oklahoma	$263.6	$57.2
Oregon	$3,079.8	$452.8
Pennsylvania	$2,597.2	$1,011.5
Rhode Island	$876.0	$128.0
South Carolina	$1,625.7	$409.3
South Dakota	$1,972.5	$197.4
Tennessee	00	
Texas	$3,913.4	$1,510.6
Vermont	$70.3	$29.9
Virginia	$1,133.6	$478.2
Washington	$1,550.5	$496.9
West Virginia	$476.6	$142.9
Wisconsin	$759.2	$335.0
Wyoming	$29.8	$7.6
Indian gaming	$41,061.2	$3,416.5
TOTAL:	$482,101.8	$39,895.5

Note: Totals may not add up because of rounding.

*Figures include parimutuel, lottery, casino and devices, bookmaking, card rooms, bingo and charitable games.

**Figures include revenue from state lotteries and private and charitable gambling interests.

USN&WR—Basic data: Harrah's Survey of Casino Entertainment; Christiansen/Cummings Associates for *International Gaming & Wagering Business*; *Amusement Business*; Major League Baseball; American Symphony Orchestra League; National Football League; League of American Theatres and Producers; New Jersey Casino Control Commission; U.S. Census Bureau; Salomon Brothers; State Capital Resource Center.

Part III

The Selling of the Lottery

Promises to the People

States tend to pass lotteries around the time politicians need to raise cash but don't want to institute anything as unpopular as a tax hike. They make all kinds of promises to slip the measures by a skeptical public: The lottery will lower taxes; it'll boost education spending; it'll save the environment. Unfortunately, these promises rarely come true. As Peter Keating points out in his *Money* magazine article, "Lotto Fever: We all lose!," "Lotteries have neither lowered taxes for their residents nor boosted funding for education, as their champions have often promised." In fact, says the article, "despite marketing slogans such as New York's 'Supporting education since 1967,' lottery states spend less of their budgets on education than do states that go without lotteries, on average."

But then, who'd ever check on them? By running lotteries, states have placed themselves in the position of promoting rather than regulating gambling. Even when a politician or two get the anti-lottery bug, they find that the money has been so tightly woven into the budget, it's almost impossible to remove. Such a situation occurred recently in California. According to a 1992 story distributed by the California Alternative News Bureau: "Last April, state Sen. Tim Leslie (R-Auburn) introduced a bill, SCA 43, that would have given voters a chance to repeal the lottery if they so desired. The bill, after being amended in the Governmental Organizations Committee to state the lottery act would not be repealed until replacement funding was found, was struck down by the Constitutional Amendments Committee in May." A spokesperson for Sen. Alfred Alquist (D- San Jose), who was originally anti-lottery, told the news service that Alquist had voted for SCA 43 until the amendment was added: "Given the current economic fiscal status of the state, to discontinue it would take money out of state coffers that we don't have." The public is being sold a bill of goods—often in the name of civic boosterism—that's getting harder and harder to undo.

Lotto Fever

We all Lose!

Peter Keating

Reprinted from the May 1996 issue of *Money*, by special permission; copyright © 1996, Time Inc.

It's 9 p.m. on a wintry Thursday night as three sweatshirt-clad New York State Lottery agents start working the crowd at a small tavern named Cavanaugh's in Blue Point, N.Y., a Long Island suburb of New York City. From their corner table at Cavanaugh's—one of 3,157 bars, restaurants and delis in which the state of New York has recently installed lottery machines—the officials schmooze with patrons, offering them baseball caps and key chains as well as free lottery tickets. They hope to persuade the crowd to play Quick Draw, a video keno—or bingo-type—game so addictive that players call it Lotto Crack.

The lottery agents don't have to do much selling. Quick Draw, displayed on three of the 10 television screens at Cavanaugh's, already has the zombie-like attention of a dozen or so customers. Players fill out cards, choosing as many as 10 numbers from 1 through 80, and then bet as much as $100 per card. When the game starts, 20 electronic balls float across the screens, landing on numbers. Players win prizes according to how many of their choices match. And win or lose, a new game begins every five minutes.

As is typically the case with lottery games, tonight most players will lose far more than they win. Cavanaugh's Quick Draw winners collect $1,250 on an average night, about half of the $2,500 spent by all the players. "I know I'm probably going to lose," says Joe Doucett, a 29-year-old electrical engineer, "but I keep playing because I might just get lucky." That, of course, is the idea.

Tempted by the possibility of turning $1 into $1 million, Doucett and his fellow gamblers throw more than $88 million every day into lottery games—more than Americans spend on all spectator sports combined. As a result, lottery sales in the District of Columbia and the 36 states that have the games soared 12.2% in 1995 to $32.1 billion, up from just $2.9 billion 15 years ago, according to the North American Association of State and Provincial Lotteries in Cleveland. (This year, New Mexico became the 37th lottery state.) What the estimated 55 million Americans who play the lottery at least once a month probably don't realize, however, is how big a rip-off the state-run games are for them as taxpayers. A six-month investigation by MONEY reveals that the lotteries have neither lowered taxes for their residents nor boosted funding for education, as their champions have often promised. What's more, by helping turn people like Andy D. into compulsive gamblers, lotteries are adding an estimated $10.9 billion a year to the financial burdens of the states and their taxpayers.

Among Our Findings:

- Lotteries are an inefficient way to raise public money. Of the $32.1 billion that states took in from lotteries last year, they kept just $11 billion—a mere third of sales—after shelling out about $21 billion on administrative costs and prizes.

- Cash-strapped states typically rely on lottery revenues to plug ever-widening budget holes rather than using the cash to lower taxes. Indeed, state spending by lottery locales (which make up 84% of the U.S. population) is projected to grow more than twice as fast in 1996 as it is in nonlottery states, according to data compiled by the National Conference of State Legislatures (NCSL) in Denver.

- Despite marketing slogans such as New York's "Supporting education since 1967," lottery states spend less of their budgets on education than do states that go without lotteries, on average. Some lottery lovers are enticed not only by the prospect of getting rich quick but also by the comforting notion that their money will go to pay for teachers and schoolbooks. But MONEY has learned that states that specifically target lottery dollars to pay for public schools often go on to decrease the share of general tax dollars budgeted to pay for education. The result: The proportion of state spending dedicated to education has remained relatively unchanged in the '90s—about 50% for lottery states and 60% for nonlottery states—despite the growth in lottery revenues. When you add it all up, the marketing claims by most state lotteries are like losing numbers on instant tickets. They seem promising at first but are disappointing once you scratch beneath the surface.

Let's Examine Some Actual Marketing Pitches:

"Giving people the choice to raise money by purchasing lottery tickets will let your state hold the line on taxes." So said Gov. Thomas Meskill of Connecticut when he successfully proposed a lottery in 1971. But despite strong lottery sales ($670.8 million last year), Connecticut state legislators enacted the state's first income tax in 1991. That's because a lottery does not inoculate a state against higher taxes. To the contrary, most states create lotteries because they need all the income they can possibly generate. That explains why, although states with lotteries have raked in more than $128 billion in ticket purchases over the past five years, average per capita taxes in those states have increased 21.7% anyway, to $1,401 a year. That growth rate is three times as high as in nonlottery states, where annual per capita taxes are now $1,049, up just 7.2% since 1990. Last year, when many state legislatures were in tax-slashing moods, your odds of seeing your taxes go up or down were pretty much the same whether or not your state had a lottery. Of the 36 states with lotteries in 1995 and Washington, D.C., 20 of them (56%) cut taxes and nine (25%) raised them, for a net tax reduction of $2.8 billion. Similarly, seven of the 14 states without lotteries (50%) reduced taxes, while only two (14%) passed increases, for an overall savings of $465 million. According to gambling industry experts, lotteries don't offer much in the way of tax relief for two reasons. First, huge as they appear, lottery sales do little to alleviate state budget problems, because state governments don't get to keep most of the proceeds. Lotteries pay a majority of revenues back to players as prizes—about 54% in 1994 (the latest year for which data are available), according to data from International Gaming & Wagering Business. Operating costs—including advertising, salaries and commissions to agents and businesses that install ticket machines—gobble up another 12¢ of every sales dollar. That leaves states with only $34.30 in profits for every $100 of lottery tickets sold. By contrast, the typical charity retains $79.80 of every $100 it raises.

What's more, states typically treat lottery revenues as "found money" that they use to close budget gaps rather than to cut taxes or spending. This year, lottery states plan to spend a total of $315 billion, or $11 billion more than they did in 1995. That's a 3.7% spending increase and matches exactly the $11 billion in profits that lottery states kept in 1995. Spending in nonlottery states, by contrast, is slated to grow just 1.46% this year, to $40.2 billion, according to NCSL. "Voters want states to spend more, and politicians look at lotteries as a way to get tax money for free," says Elizabeth Davis, policy analyst at the Center for the Study of the States in Albany, N.Y.

"We are going to need new money if we want to have good schools. Either we have a huge tax bill or we approve a lottery." That's what then Gov. Ann Richards told her fellow Texans in a televised address the day before the state voted to establish a lottery in 1991. Money for education is the explicit or implicit promise that most lottery promoters make: 18 states specifically earmark lottery money for education, and most others claim that schools benefit from the games. Says Mary Fulton, a policy analyst at the Education Commission of the States in Denver: "There's a deep and widespread perception among the public that lottery revenues are being used to substantially fund education."

During this decade, however, states with lotteries actually dedicated a declining share of their total spending to schools. In 1994 (the latest year for which data are available), lottery states devoted 49% of their total spending to education, down slightly from 50.1% in 1990, according to the Center for the Study of the States. Meanwhile, over the same time period, the average budget share for education increased slightly for nonlottery states, from 58.2% to 58.9%. Florida, which created its lottery in 1988 to "enhance education," is one of several states that claim to earmark lottery money for schools but in reality mix it with general funds, so it's next to impossible to know where the money goes. This year Florida plans to spend just $114 million, or 14%, of its projected $829 million in lottery profits on specific statewide education projects. The other $715 million will be sucked into the general budget.

"We've been hurt by our lottery," says Gary Landry, spokesman for the Florida Education Association, the local school employees' union. "The state has simply replaced general revenues with lottery money—at a time when enrollments are increasing. It's a big shell game."

In New York State, lottery profits ($1.24 billion in 1995) are earmarked by law for education, and the phrase "Supporting education since 1967" appears on the back of every Quick Draw play card. The truth: Education funding is set by the state legislature and does not automatically rise with lottery sales. "If they want to use half the money to plug a hole in the budget, there's nothing to say they can't," says Bill Pape, spokesman for the New York State School Boards Association. "Once it's in the general fund, it can be used for anything."

"The benefits of the lottery far exceed the social costs." These are the words of Jeff Perlee, director of the New York Lottery. Wanna bet? The odds are that you will pick up some of the estimated $10.9 billion tab run up by the 1.5% to 7% of lottery gamblers who lose self-control from compulsive wagering. Robert Goodman, professor of public policy at Hampshire College in Amherst, Mass. and author of *The Luck Business* [Free Press, $23], conservatively pegs the annual cost to the

U.S. economy of each additional problem gambler at $13,200. Reasons for the hefty price tag: Compulsive gamblers are more likely than healthy consumers to attempt suicide, destroy their families, write bad checks, embezzle money, go bankrupt and land in court or jail.

The proportion of callers to the Trenton, N.J.-based Council on Compulsive Gambling's national hotline who say they're addicted to lotteries has risen from 16% to 43% over the past decade. And the problem of compulsive lottery gambling seems destined to rise, as states offer more and more quick-action games. "If anyone thinks that putting lotteries and video terminals on every block won't lead to addictive and criminal behavior, they're in outer space," says Dr. Valerie Lorenz, director of the Compulsive Gambling Center in Baltimore. "We saw keno addicts within two weeks after it was introduced in Maryland." Even some state lottery officials agree. "Problem gambling was not apparent in Oregon before the state took video lotteries out of back rooms and turned them into a public experience," admits David Hooper, public affairs manager for that state's lottery.

Currently, state governments are spending more than $350 million a year to market a new wave of especially addictive instant-jackpot lottery games. Oregon, Rhode Island, South Dakota and West Virginia, for example, have legalized video lottery terminals, which blur the lines between lotteries and slot machines, generating $3.8 billion in sales last year alone. Keno games similar to New York's 12-games-an-hour Quick Draw are now available in 13 states and produced more than $1.6 billion in sales in 1995. "It's a consistent pattern," says public policy professor Robert Goodman. "Revenues are never able to meet the demands of the states over time, so they raise the stakes of the games. The states are the real addicts."

What You Should Do

Here Are Three Tips for Taxpayers:

- Find out how your state is using its lottery money. Call your state lottery commission or department of revenue, and ask how lottery revenues are allocated. Inquire whether lottery money is being used to replace general fund spending on schools, and find out if plans exist to expand your state's lottery games. If you don't like what you hear, write to your governor and state legislators and let them know.

- If you or someone you know is having trouble controlling spending on lotteries, get help. You can call the National Council on Problem Gambling (800-522-4700), a nonprofit agency whose staffers will refer you to local counselors and meetings.

- If you live in a state with an income tax and want to help its fiscal health while profiting at the same time, consider investing in your state's tax-free municipal bonds. Today, such bonds—yielding about 4.65% to 5.75%—often pay more after taxes than taxable alternatives such as bank CDs for people in the 28% tax bracket or higher (married couples with taxable incomes above $40,100 and singles with incomes above $24,000). Since the odds of winning a standard lotto jackpot are 1 in 13.8 million, according to James Walsh, author of *True Odds* [Merritt, $19.95], your chances of making money are substantially higher with muni bonds than they are with lottery tickets.

The Sting

Millions of Losers Every Week

How the State Lottery Became the Worst Bet in Town

Jennifer Vogel
City Pages, August 4, 1993

"What are your luckies?" A middle-age woman is standing in a downtown skyway convenience store, her 15-year-old son in tow. Behind them a large black Lotto America machine spits out tickets without pause while lights race across the front promising "100 MILLION $100 MILLION $100 MILLION." The kid thinks for a minute and whispers conspiratorially to his mother, who scribbles a series of numbers onto a Powerball ticket and steps up to the counter.

Just a few days earlier, in a tiny Minnesota town along the Mississippi, a 40-ish man walked into a bar, bellied up and ordered a beer. "I don't care what anyone says. If I win, I'm never going to work another day in my life," he pledged to the elderly bartender, who'd heard it before. "It's just ridiculous what people say, that they are going to keep working. I would quit my job. I'd call in rich."

Powerball is everywhere. Newspapers and TV stations have no qualms about ordaining it as big news; they dutifully show up each day to shoot the long lines of would-be millionaires puzzling over just the right combination of digits. Birthdays, anniversaries, and lucky numbers from childhood are getting quite a workout.

Some nobody will beat the long odds—55 million to one—and win the jackpot. Will become somebody. Even after the drawing is over, the magic doesn't wear off. Crowds gather early the next day at the Sentry Food Store-South in Fond du Lac, Wisconsin, to get a glimpse of the man who bought *the* ticket, a 30-year-old school teacher who spends his first few days as a millionaire avoiding the public eye.

When Minnesota was deciding to have a state lottery—through a 1988 constitutional amendment and 1989 legislation—its promoters worked hard to create the impression that it would be good for the state. And that a lot of money would go to the environment and to creating jobs in outstate Minnesota. The way it ended up, very little of each dollar spent on lottery tickets actually goes to the environment and none goes to rural business. That contradiction is due in part to the misleading way politicians and media portrayed the issue in the first place and in part because the Legislature keeps tinkering with the revenue pie.

The lottery continues to trade on the perception that a ton of money is being funneled into the environment to promote ticket sales. Actually, the amount is only about 7 cents of each of the nearly 300 million dollars the lottery took in last year. But that doesn't stop the lottery from churning out pieces like the poster that depicts two fishermen sitting on a peaceful pond at sunset. The tagline: "Helping Minnesota Enjoy the Good Life." The lottery logo, of course, is a loon. Yet Lottery Director George Andersen contends that where the money goes is not his concern. "It's not up to me," he says. "It's not my job. I've got plenty to worry about without doing that. I like to be able to point with pride to projects, I mean, that helps. And we do that."

It's hard to argue that helping the environment is the main reason people play. As state Rep. Jim Rice (DFL-Mpls.), a long-time critic of the lottery, puts it: "How many people do you think when they were out to win that $100 million prize went in there because they thought they were going to preserve one chickadee?" But it has a lot to do with why the lottery was established here in the first place.

Andersen—a large friendly man who's quick with a funny story, is sitting behind a very tidy, expensive-looking desk. Andersen himself appears informal—his jacket slung over the back of his chair, his identification tag often tangling with his tie. To visitors, he offers Tootsie Rolls from a large jar on his desk. But Andersen's easy manner belies an acute consciousness of how he and the lottery appear to outsiders. He all but refuses to give our photographer a casual pose. And he manages to talk around some of the more critical questions asked.

Andersen pops antacids the whole time we're talking. He's trying to quit smoking, he says, but admits it isn't going too well. Now he drinks more coffee, which means more bathroom trips, he explains—and more chances to step out for a cigarette.

Andersen, who left as second in command of the Pennsylvania lottery almost four years ago to take over Minnesota's has a philosophy about promoting the game. "The business of lottery is not about winning," he says. "It's about entertaining and having fun. Because most people don't win. I mean, they need to win frequently and so on as a reinforcement. But it's an entertainment vehicle that makes money."

What, if not winning, is the entertainment value?

"Dreams. And the anticipation of winning. It's the anticipation of a dramatic lifestyle change. It's exciting. The anticipation is what it's all about."

Jim Rice thinks Andersen is a throwback. "He looks to me like the front man at the carnival. Don't get me wrong," he adds, "I like the guy. But if he weren't running our lottery, I think he's got the character to sell the Brooklyn Bridge." In a sense, selling the lottery is a lot like selling the Brooklyn Bridge. Even Andersen admits it offers just about the worst odds in town, with only a 65 percent pay-out rate. Blackjack pays out around 98 cents on the dollar, while slots pay 92. Even pulltabs have an 80 percent pay-out rate.

By definition, the lottery is a strange animal. It is, at root, a public agency, with its proceeds going to the state and its director chosen by the governor. Yet you'd never catch the head of any other state agency getting a $44,500 bonus on a $75,500 annual salary. (After a public outcry, Andersen declined to accept it and the power to award bonuses was taken away from the lottery board of directors.)

The lottery shares the mission of a private company—to turn a profit. Toward that end, lottery promotions fill billboards and airwaves. The idea is to convince people that scratching tickets is fun. The 9 to 10 television commercials and 15 to 20 radio spots developed every year usually have a harmless, festive edge and feature characters like talking ants. That's in part because state law prohibits the money-falling-from-the-sky type commercials often seen in other states. A recent TV ad shown locally features a man sticking himself to a bus with magnets touting the phrase "fun has many nuances." Andersen repeats the words like a mantra after showing the commercial on video in his office. The lottery spent just under $8 million on advertising last year, he says.

Minnesota themes go over well, like Lakes and Loons, Our Minnesota and Cabin Fever. Playing off state pride, they depict the likes of lakes, farmhouses, tractors, and animals. Of course, Andersen *is* from out of state and makes a mistake now and again. Mosquito Madness, for example, wasn't a big seller. "It was a funny caricature of a mosquito with an aviator's hat on," he shrugs. "Apparently people really don't like mosquitoes."

Novelty is enough to sell a lottery in the beginning. Now that that's worn off, Andersen tries to deliver a more potent fix: more and more games. In the first year there were nine games. This year there will be 14 to 16. And he's decided to have more than one game for sale at a time and to offer some tickets at $2 or $5 a piece so larger prizes are available. Another way to keep people playing is to offer games with varying odds and pay-out structures. Beat the Dealer, for instance, boasts of "four games on one ticket!" So your chances of winning are four times as great right? Wrong. In fact, Beat the Dealer features worse odds than most games the state's done: The chances of winning even a dollar are only one in 10.

Besides recruiting players, the lottery recruits stores, which get close to 6 cents for every ticket sold—only a penny less than goes to the environment. They're encouraged to come up with homegrown lottery promotions. Some hold "losers drawings" or "second chance drawings" for T-shirts and other novelty items. Just sign your losing tickets and put them in the box. Others get more creative. At the Econofoods in Winona, for example, they reportedly increased lottery sales by 590 percent for a short period of time a few months ago by putting tickets in with pre-packaged meats, hanging plants, roasted chickens, and freshly baked pies.

Getting shoppers to purchase scratch-off dreams wasn't the first bit of peddling done on behalf of the lottery. It had to be approved by the voters and the legislature first.

In 1988-89, Minnesota was just coming of age as far as gambling was concerned. There was already charitable gaming and parimutuel betting, but Indian gaming hadn't entered the picture yet. "When the lottery passed," remembers state Representative Karen Clark (DFL-Mpls.) who voted against it, "it changed the tone. It became OK for public dollars to be raised through gambling and private gambling gained more acceptance and credibility." Clark says when Canterbury Downs died, it didn't look like Minnesotans were gamblers, "but I guess that was wrong."

Gambling in the state increased tenfold between 1985 and 1991. In 1985, gross receipts were estimated at slightly under $200 million. By 1990, that number had increased to $2 billion. Andersen notes that Minnesota has the highest per capita pulltab play in the country. "Something like a quarter of all charitable gambling in North America is in Minnesota," he says, adding that Minnesota ranks third in total per capita dollars spent on gambling, behind only Nevada and New Jersey.

Besides dollars spent, there are other indicators that the gambling business is booming—such as an increase in the number of compulsive gamblers. The state does give a small amount every year to treatment—$450,000 was earmarked in 1992 for "compulsive gambling and public safety."

Dennis Slater of Gambler's Choice, a gambling addiction group, points out one major difference between lottery players and other gamblers: Income level. "They are either middle income or lower," he says. "They don't have the money to play the big games." That's in line with what studies in other states have shown. But Andersen heartily denies that poor people in Minnesota spend a higher portion of their income than anybody else on it: "In Minnesota the discretionary income level is very, very high. During Powerball week, we sold $5.8 million worth of tickets in four days. There was a newspaper article that said only the poor people are playing. If the poor are playing, by definition they aren't poor, because they spent $5.8 million dollars in four days.

"People with discretionary dollars. That's all we go after. We don't solicit [the poor] and we don't target them. Nor do we ignore them. We do advertise in minority media a lot. It's the right thing to do."

Rice sees it differently. "The poorest neighborhoods are where the most tickets are sold," he says flatly, citing the lottery's own sales figures—which show Near North Minneapolis spending over $6.5 million on tickets last year, while [the upscale suburb of] Edina spent $593,962. "And there were big sales around Rice Street and West 7th St. in St. Paul. It's the poorest people, with the least discretionary money, who are buying the tickets."

"We knew this before the lottery passed," concurs Clark. "All the research showed what would probably happen. It's one issue that I find myself at odds with my constituency on. Many of them love it."

Andersen says he's not familiar with the numbers Rice cites. When pressed, he says: "It depends on whether people were there playing and what percentage of the population they would be and if there is a commuter path through there where people could stop at a [convenience] store. One of our best areas is in Plymouth."

The lottery's status as a regressive tax hardly dented the public debate while it was being shepherded through the referendum process and the Legislature. Its architects managed to deflect that heat by packaging the lottery to look good to potential opponents. For one thing, recalls Clark, "It was being sold as a way to preserve the environment. And one of the ways the lottery got passed with rural members who were skeptical was that some of the money was supposed to go to rural development."

Though most news accounts of the lottery push focused on the diversion of funds to the environment, then Governor Rudy Perpich's biggest concern, according to a former staffer, was to create jobs. His father had been an erratically employed iron-ore miner on the Iron Range; he saw the decline of mining and knew that emerging industry wouldn't be beating a path to northern Minnesota to replace these jobs. So he got involved in the Greater Minnesota Corporation—a public/private partnership conceived in 1987 and designed to encourage long-term economic development in outstate Minnesota.

But for Perpich, getting money for the GMC from the legislature was worse than pulling teeth. Legislators would exploit GMC funding requests to make the governor compromise on other programs. When the lottery proposal came along, Perpich saw the source of funding he'd been waiting for. He traveled all over the state, grandstanding in small town after small town. He lobbied rural legislators. He pushed hard—in some cases threatening business interests that if they wanted any money at all from the Legislature in the near future, they had better support the lottery.

According to one former administration insider, Perpich started pledging lottery proceeds to the Environment and Natural Resources Trust Fund mainly because he needed more support to get the lottery passed. "The environment was not nearly as important to him as the Greater Minnesota Corporation," he says. "Adding the environmental trust fund was as much a design to broaden support for the lottery as to improve the environment. He knew that if he brought in the trust fund, he would broaden his coalition. Business and environment are usually diametrically opposed. So in bringing them together he created a coalition out of people who might otherwise be enemies. That was crucial to its passage."

He went to state Representative Willard Munger, an elder legislator who had made the environment his main legislative project. The environmental trust fund was his baby and at first, says the former administration official, "Willard didn't want his trust fund contaminated with the lottery. He didn't want this pristine thing attached to a vice. But the governor finally said, 'Willard, there is no other way to fund it.' Willard did end up supporting it, and once he did, it helped. People respected him as an elder statesman. He brought on the fringe people that probably made the difference. He had the idea that if we are going to have something bad, let's make it do some good."

That was the line of reasoning the governor promoted. According to the official, lobbyists told legislators that the lottery "was probably going to pass anyway. Our argument was that if you are on the fence, if you get to a point where you…need a justification, at least you could join the governor, who didn't want it either. If it had to pass, at least it could be for these public purposes."

The public and most legislators alike were sold on the idea. They could vote for a lottery with a clear conscience because the profits would go to two very worthy causes—half to the environment and half to rural business. But despite all the rhetoric, only about 18.3 cents out of every dollar goes to the lottery's beneficiaries. Of that sum, 40 percent (or about 7 cents) goes to the environment and 60 percent (or about 11 cents) to the state's general fund. None is earmarked for rural business development anymore.

Jim Rice doubts the lottery would pass if the vote were held today. As evidence he cites a recent bill to open another horse racing track, which garnered only 45 votes. He says the "surprisingly low amount of support" for the bill signifies a fear that gambling has gotten out of control in the state. "It was a very surprising vote. People feel they've opened a Pandora's box. Some legislators have told me they regretted the vote they made on the lottery." According to Rice, there are currently two bills in the legislature to repeal it.

Everyone has seen the familiar oval picture of a loon floating stoically on a lake backed by trees and a sunset that is the lottery's logo. And it's been hard to miss their motto: "Proceeds benefit our natural and economic environments."

But sometimes people get curious about where the money goes, exactly. Current and wanna-be public officials say they hear that question often when they go door to door campaigning. It's easy to understand the confusion. Since the lottery's passage, the legislature hasn't stopped reorganizing the proceeds pie. According to official figures from fiscal year 1992, 57.8 cents of every dollar spent on the lottery was given out in prizes. The legislative mandate for prize payouts has risen to 60 percent this year, and Andersen says he expects to exceed that by about 5 percent. (In 1992, the lottery exceeded its mandated payout by 2.8 percent.) Of the rest, 18.5 cents went to the beneficiaries, 11.6 cents to operating expenses; 6.5 cents was returned to the state in the form of a sales tax and 5.8 cents went to commissions and incentives to retailers.

How did it get that way? First, the Legislature cut money tagged for the environment from 50 percent of proceeds to 40 percent and they cut funding for rural business and development from 50 percent to 25 percent. The other 35 percent was supposed to go to higher education and environmental and natural resources. But it wasn't long before that slice of the pie was diverted to the state's general fund, where officials can spend it as they see fit. Soon the GMC lost its final 25 percent and that share was added to the general fund, giving it the lion's share of lottery proceeds—60 percent.

The reduction in funding to the environmental trust fund to 40 percent was a compromise; in return, that funding level was locked in for 10 years via state constitutional amendment. (Amendments are harder to change than simple statutes, because they must be put to a public vote.)

The GMC's funding cutoff is a more convoluted story. According to the administration official "Perpich shared the GMC with Senator [Roger] Moe. The team was Moe and [Rudy] Perpich. In the 1988 legislative session, nobody knew whether Perpich would run again, and Moe wanted to be governor. [Perpich's Commerce Commissioner] Mike Hatch was making all kinds of noises about wanting to be governor. Roger told Perpich to make him quit it. That breached the friendship between Roger and Rudy.

"Then Terry Montgomery left as the governor's chief of staff in September of '87. He took over the GMC, which made sense because he was Rudy's most trusted person. So Terry's got Roger and Rudy as allies going into the '88 session to get money. When they had their falling out, Terry was caught in the middle. He had to decide who his allegiance was with. Terry sided with Roger, and Rudy took a hike from [the GMC]. He stopped pushing it at the Legislature and didn't believe it would do what he wanted it to anymore. Then Terry got involved in a harassment issue and the whole thing was drawn into question. It was a terribly unfortunate thing. That was followed by an audit of the GMC, and it was learned that Terry had misused funds. And then the Legislature took a hike from it. Even Roger."

The 40 percent of lottery profits that go to the Environment and Natural Resources Trust Fund amounted to just under $22 million in 1992 and just under $27 million in '91. But even that money isn't being spent in the ways those pictures of loons might conjure. It's committed to a bank account for 10 years, where it's being invested in stocks and bonds. Little more than the interest off that fund, which is about 10 percent, or a grand total of $14.9 million for the last biennium is actually being spent on the environment. The money that does get doled out by the Legislative Commission on Minnesota Resources (LCMR) goes almost exclusively to government agencies like the Department of Natural Resources. And many of the 29 projects funded so far consist of mapping and database-gathering. Smaller environmental groups who may be doing more hands-on innovative things tend not to have the resources or time to sit through the LCMR's rigorous, time-consuming funding process. (State Representative Phyllis Kahn, who chairs the LCMR, says the process takes two years.) Yet Lisa Doerr from Citizens for a Better Environment says when people from her group go door to door asking for donations, people often want to know, "Why don't you just get it from the lottery?"

Back in 1988, Rice teamed up with former governor Al Quie, flying all over the state to combat the proposed lottery.

Rice made some predictions at the time—mainly that the legislature would reduce the amount committed to the environment and job creation. So he's not surprised at the way things turned out. The selling of the lottery, he says, was all about putting a noble face on a revenue-generating plan. "Whatever the state's needs for money," he says, "they shouldn't be so strong that you go out and bilk your own people to get it. The promise to the people, the covenant, was that 50 percent would be spent on the environment and 50 percent would go to business development."

Now he has another prediction, this one about the future of the environmental trust fund: "In another seven or eight years, when the trust fund is due, I think all the money will end up going to the general fund. And bozos like me will get to decide how it will be spent—any way we please."

Scratch & Sniffle

Talking odds is pretty abstract. What does it mean, in cold hard cash for example, to have a one in 5.75 chance of winning a dollar, a one in 40,000 chance of winning $1,000? To find out, we purchased 50 tickets from a south Minneapolis convenience store. We chose Our Minnesota since it's one of the newer games and appears to be a big seller.

Getting the tickets turned out to be a chore in itself. Upon handing the clerk a check, we found out it was no good as far as the lottery was concerned. According to Minnesota law, game tickets have to be paid for in cash. "Or people will write checks for $500 thinking they are going to win the jackpot," the clerk explained, "and they don't. Then it turns out they don't have that much in their account." Okay. We got the cash and the tickets.

The goal of Our Minnesota is to scratch and match three of the same number and you win that amount. Prizes range from $1 to $10,000. The odds are one in 3.93 of winning one of these dollar amounts. That means that approximately 25 percent of the tickets in this game are winners, right?

Let's see. We got out our penny and scratched. The first

two numbers we uncovered looked promising—two $10,000 characters. That combination, along with a double $1,000 on a ticket, came up a lot. It became more and more obvious, since only one of our losing tickets had two $1 or two $3 on them, that the losing combinations were chosen carefully to make players feel like they just missed the big jackpot. Some marketing executive somewhere figured out that people are more likely to buy another ticket that way. All but 8 of our losing tickets had two $1,000 or two $10,000 on them. Eleven had both combinations.

Not surprisingly, we never won $10,000. In fact no single ticket we scratched even yielded $10. Thirteen of our 50 tickets were winners—almost exactly what the odds predict. Nine paid us $1. Three paid us $3. And one paid us $5. The total return on our investment? A grand total of $23.

You Lose!

The Sad Truth
About the Texas Lottery

Robert Draper
Texas Monthly, June 1993

On April 8, 1993, the Texas lottery's traveling carnival made its twenty-first stop on its statewide tour and pitched tent in the ballroom of the Odessa Holiday Inn Centre. By six in the evening, the ballroom was filled to capacity with Odessa's salt of the earth—the very young and the very old, all races represented, some folks in wheelchairs and others jumping in the aisles. They were cheering and chatting, rising to the oratorical bait of the man standing onstage with a microphone in his hand and wearing a phony $100 bill fashioned into a bow tie. He was Sonny Melendrez, a San Antonio radio personality and the lottery's emcee, and his monologue owed a great debt to the rhetoric of game show hosts, televangelists, and snake oil salesmen. "This is the biggest crowd the lottery *has ever seen*! Did you know that the Texas Lottery is the biggest lottery *in the world*? In the Texas Lottery *everyone is a winner*! And in just a minute, one of these seven individuals seated right here will win *one million dollars*!"

Each of these statements was untrue, even the part about the $1 million, as the Internal Revenue Service would snatch up $280,000 of the sum before the winner ever laid a hand on the big check. But no one was here to gather facts. Today was a day for daring to dream, and the more myths, the merrier. The state was offering an unconditional guarantee: If you walked into this ballroom, you would see a miracle take place. You would watch an average Joe, one of your own kind, become instantly rich.

Behind Melendrez, seated on a stage adorned with faux cacti and faux barbed wire, the seven finalists squirmed on brightly colored chairs. They were young and old, black and white and Hispanic; the seven of them represented an astoundingly accurate cross section of the 1,500 people in the audience. The implications were almost overpowering. Ah, but what made these seven so special? Luck, magic, destiny, call it what you will—and the fact that each of them had bought a Lone Star Millionaire instant lottery ticket, scratched off the surface, and discovered the word "entry" printed three times or a single star on the ticket. They had mailed off their tickets to the Texas Lottery and later, they had received a phone call from a state official informing them that their ticket had been one of the seven randomly selected for the upcoming grand prize drawing. In a few moments each finalist would select one of the cowboy hats hanging on the faux cactus hat rack; a number had been taped inside each hat. Five of those numbers would match five numbers randomly selected from the lottery hopper. Two of the finalists who held those numbers would win $10,000, another two would win $15,000, and one would win $25,000. The two finalists whose numbers were not drawn from the hopper would then stand in front of two plastic vaults. Within one of the vaults was a cardboard check for $50,000. In the other vault was the grand prize: $1 million, before taxes. Luck or magic or destiny would see the finalists through to their respective prizes. But to have gotten this far, each of them had to have spent at least $1 playing the lottery, and the audience understood this. Perhaps they even understood that, for a million-dollar prize to become possible, some two million lottery tickets would have to be sold—sold, one might suppose, to folks such as the 1,500 dreamers beholding a single individual's turn of fortune.

But even a cynic is susceptible to dreams. As luck would have it, the man whose number entitled him to the plastic vault that contained a cardboard check for $1 million happened to be Doyle Norton, a 24-year-old unmarried lawn-service worker from Mesquite. Throughout the festivities, Norton had been the most stoic of the seven; he had seemed almost determined to find no thrill in any of it. But when he opened the safe and discovered its contents, his body went limp and his face flushed with astonishment. As the ballroom thundered with joy, he threw his cowboy hat into the air and lurched about the stage like a child transported to wonderland. For whatever had befallen him in the past, Doyle Norton was, at that moment, the luckiest man on earth; thereafter no one could say that Doyle Norton was a stranger to fortune. And for that matter, no one in the audience could say they had never watched a dream come true. Quite the contrary: Not only had they seen it, but its methodology was revealed to them. One ticket, $1 million. "Throw your hat again for the video camera!" Sonny Melendrez yelled, and Norton obliged, again and then again. The Odessa crowd stayed for every fling of the hat, cheering until the winner left the stage and there was nothing left to cheer.

The newest billion-dollar industry to come to Texas is one year old as of May 29 and has so thoroughly insinuated itself that it taxes the memory to recall when Texans weren't scratching away at little pieces of paper or conjuring up six numbers at a time. In its first year the lottery has achieved gross sales of $1.8 billion, 40 percent of which has been deposited in the state's general revenue fund. More than 11 million Texans have played the lottery. The game's luckiest player, a 65-year-old retired nurse from Schulenburg, won a $21.7 million jackpot; its most ignominious loser is a Houston convenience store clerk who is serving a sentence of four years in prison for stealing 7,500 tickets. Between these two extremes dwell nearly two billion wins and losses, with a tale to accompany every dream consummated and every hope shot to hell.

The lottery has produced its own culture, one that might stir the reminiscences of Texans who lived the early years of the oil boom. New words—"lotto," "scratch-off," "roll-over"—have crept into the vocabulary; in icehouses and convenience stores across the state, adults congregate and find themselves discussing lucky numbers, the hottest retail outlet, and the size of the latest jackpot. As in the oil culture, there are dabblers and high rollers, big-time winners and pathetic types who gamble all they've got. The lottery has created jobs for some, destroyed the lives of others. And the men and women in charge of the state lottery share a familiar obsession: If they have their way, Texas will be the nation's lottery capital, the biggest in the industry.

The comparisons with the oil-boom culture end there. In the mythology of the oil patch, a wildcatter's savvy and determination could gain him the upper hand over dumb luck; in the ways of the lottery, a player is entirely at its mercy. Nothing about the lottery is uniquely Texan. If anything, the lottery era in its infancy has succeeded in turning the petro-ethic on its head. Now that the state can no longer stake its fortune on the labors of a few independent-minded winners, it seeks its profit from the 11 million Texans whom the state has converted into losers.

Yet the new era comes to us fashionably cloaked. If there is such a thing as a politically correct lottery, it resides in Texas. The state's model relies less on government bureaucrats and more on the private sector than practically any other lottery in the world. Its director, Nora Linares, is a Hispanic woman. She and other state officials take pleasure in pointing out that their advertisements, by legislative mandate, do not "unduly influence" the public. The lottery tickets themselves are the first ever to be fully biodegradable and recyclable. Innovations notwithstanding, however, Texas has a lottery for precisely the same reason that 35 other states and dozens of other nations have lotteries. Says Bill Bergman, the executive director of the North American Association of State and Provincial Lotteries: "Lotteries are driven totally by economic needs and by the failure of state legislatures to impose taxes to meet those needs." Texas did not get a lottery when Texans first indicated through public opinion polls that they wanted one—that was years beforehand; the lottery came to Texas only when Texas politicians needed fast money. It's easy to forget that, just as it's easy to think of the lottery as a token of the government's generosity, as state-sponsored fun and games. But as with an unscratched lottery ticket, there is more—or rather, less—than meets the eye.

From the outset, the lottery has depended on a series of deceptions, large and small, beginning with the reason for its existence. First, our elected officials convinced us that the lottery was the only way out of a tax increase, though fiscal projections had made it abundantly clear that higher taxes were inevitable anyway. Next, lottery officials sought to promote the lottery as wholesome recreation, a pastime that did no one any harm—a "painless tax," though evidence was widespread that those who would bear the brunt of the tax would be working-class Texans. And finally, while reminding us that the lottery was a "voluntary tax," the lottery and the Legislature joined hands in an exhaustive, spare-no-expense effort to barrage Texans with enticements: a new carefully researched gimmick every month, a new promotional blitz with every game, billboards, newsletters, and press conferences with instant millionaires, so that our wallets might never close and we might never awaken from our Doyle Norton dreams.

Deception 1. A Necessary Tax
(Or, The Economy, Stupid)

"If there is a single person most responsible for the Texas Lottery," says former anti-gambling lobbyist Sue Cox, "it's James Carville."

In 1987 the political guru who masterminded Bill Clinton's 1992 presidential campaign blueprinted the Kentucky gubernatorial campaign of Wallace Wilkinson, a dark horse Democrat with a single cause: passage of a state lottery. To everyone's astonishment, Wilkinson upset former governor John Y. Brown. Two years later, when Texas attorney general Jim Mattox decided to run for governor of the state, he brought in Carville as a strategist. Carville urged Mattox to ponder the lessons learned from the Kentucky race. Mattox's campaign manager, Jim Cunningham, was in no position to dissuade Mattox, since it was Cunningham who had managed Brown's losing campaign in 1987.

The whole notion didn't sit well with Mattox: He was a Baptist and had consistently sided with anti-gambling groups. But Mattox was burning to be governor. With the Texas Supreme Court's ruling that demanded a costly overhaul of the public-school finance system, every politician in the state knew a tax increase was inevitable, and each of them was searching for a way to avoid saying so to the voters. If Mattox didn't seize the lottery issue for himself, someone else might. On October 10, 1989, the attorney general declared his candidacy and proclaimed himself "the only candidate who has come out for the lottery and opposed new taxes." Before long, Mattox was presenting the issue as a choice between a lottery and higher taxes.

The ruse was as old as the lottery itself. The first two lotteries to pass through state legislatures in the modern era (New Hampshire in 1964 and New York in 1967) did so after the public was told that a lottery would spare them from tax hikes. Still, taxes have gone up in most of the 35 states that have lotteries—the simple reason being that lotteries cannot come close to satisfying government's lust for money. As a case in point, the lottery that generates the most revenue in the nation happens to reside in tax-crazy Massachusetts.

Mattox doubtless knew all this. And though polls showed, year in and year out, that Texans favored an end to the constitutional ban on a lottery that dated back to 1845, the state's citizens weren't losing any sleep over the matter. Since 1982 five lottery bills had died in committee with barely a murmur of public displeasure. "Most politicians felt that, despite the polls, there were political dangers to the lottery," says David Hudson, a former state representative from Tyler who led the legislative coalition against the lottery. "It was a volatile issue, like the wet-dry issue, and you ran the risk of drawing the animosity of church groups."

But Mattox, the consummate political bulldog, was just the candidate to ramrod the lottery issue into the public debate. How Democratic rival Ann Richards reacted to Mattox's crusade could be viewed as a case study in political opportunism. Like her opponent, Richards was predisposed against lotteries. As state treasurer in 1985, she had initiated a study of lotteries in other states following a proposal that would place a Texas lottery under the state treasury's umbrella. The unpredictability of the revenue flow—interest in a lottery tends to fade after the first year or two—coupled with the security risks, left Richards feeling uneasy. But five days after Mattox launched his candidacy, she revealed an even deeper concern on a Dallas television show. "What happens in every state in which there is a lottery," Richards said, "is that the sales are concentrated in the poorest communities, because it is those people who are willing to take the gamble to win big. And in my heart of hearts, I just could not buy into a system that really was going to be marketing a program of chance to people who are poor and could ill afford to buy those tickets."

Yet as Mattox's lottery-or-taxes rhetoric intensified, Richards grew less attentive to her heart of hearts and started worrying about voters who bought Mattox's line and wanted to know why Richards preferred mandatory taxes over a voluntary one. Her opposition began to soften. By the end of the primary, she was all in favor of a lottery. Richards survived the brawl with Mattox, and in the fall campaign against Republican Clayton Williams, she didn't wait to be asked about her lottery stance. By enthusiastically declaring her support, Ann Richards was telling the people what they wanted to hear—but more important, she was avoiding telling the people what they didn't want to hear.

The legislative vote on a constitutional amendment permitting the lottery ironically was Governor Richards' first test of leadership. By now, lottery passage was her pet issue, not Mattox's or Carville's. She hit the hustings with gusto, dismissing what she now called the "myths" about the lottery's ill effects, reminding the faint of heart, "The bottom line is money for Texas," and adding, with populist grandeur, "The moral choice is to allow the people of the state to decide." In early 1991 Richards met with leaders of the local horse- and dog-racing industries, which stood to lose business should a lottery be introduced. The newly elected governor offered them the carrot or the stick. If you stay out of the fight, she told them, I'll support a reduction in your taxes. But if you try to defeat the lottery, I will fight you. The racetrack interests shut their mouths and got their tax cuts.

The anti-lottery forces, led by Sue Cox of Texans Who Care, Weston Ware of the Christian Life Commission, and former state legislator David Hudson, were just as tenacious as Richards. On February 25, 1991, the lottery initiative fell ten votes shy of the two-thirds House vote needed to place it on the May ballot. An icy Richards told the press, "Today, with their no vote, fifty-six members have assured the necessity of a sizable tax bill."

The fight, it turned out, was not lost; it had just been premature. The fiscal crisis hadn't fully ripened. The Legislature's regular session ended in May without producing a state budget, and lawmakers were waiting hopefully for spending cuts to be proposed by comptroller John Sharp. By midsummer, however, it was apparent that some of Sharp's reductions were politically unpalatable, and the desperate search for money was on again. House Speaker Gib Lewis picked up where Richards had left off: "There's going to be either a tremendous tax bill," he said, "or a lottery. That's the choice they have." On the morning of August 10, a Senate filibuster fizzled out, and the lottery referendum was placed on the November ballot. By the end of the year, the referendum had passed—so had a $2.6 billion tax increase.

Deception 2. A Fun Tax

Here it comes
Don't you love that lucky feeling
Oh it's fun
To anticipate that feeling
It could happen any minute
You could be the one to win it
When you play the game of Texas
Here's the fun
So get out there and get in it
'Cause somebody's gonna win it
When you play the game of Texas
Here's the fun

—the Texas Lottery jingle

There is nothing fun about the Texas headquarters of GTECH, the Rhode Island company that runs the Texas Lottery. The building is an unmarked brick structure in northeast Austin. The doors to its reception lobby are locked, and the comings and goings of employees are monitored by cameras, motion detectors, and recording devices. The building's primary feature is the control room, which could have been designed by NASA. Technicians and computer operators sit quietly among hulking Digital Equipment mainframes, rows and rows of terminals, overhead monitors flashing technical data, and telephones that connect this room to more than 20,000 retail units across Texas. The atmosphere in the control room suggest precision, solemnity; here one finds the lottery's dark side.

In the office of GTECH general manager Jim Hosker, there is a computer monitor that displays a number representing the day's Texas Lottery sales. The number changes every four seconds; every four seconds, Texans pump hundreds of dollars into the lottery. None of this surprises Hosker. He is an industry lifer, the coinventor of the instant scratch-off ticket and a former director of both the Massachusetts and the Kentucky lotteries. In 1992 GTECH, as it often does, lured the public official into the private sector to run the firm's Texas Lottery operations. The 62-year-old executive says that he is paid between $100,000 and $200,000, and that after his work is done here, he'll retire to Boston.

GTECH and Hosker aren't here to have fun. In fact, GTECH policy forbids employees to play the lottery. Their sole mission is to make money, both for themselves and for the state, and they expect to make a lot of it. By the time the five-year contract—the largest in the country because of its privatized structure—expires in 1997, GTECH has estimated that it will gross more than $405 million from its 3.944 percent cut of the state lottery pie. Once you understand how much money is involved, the remarks of the gruff, silver-haired Bostonian are less jolting, and highly illuminating. When Hosker says, "The first week after start-up the players will buy any ticket they can get their hands on," he is revealing why the Texas Lottery's first instant game offered the rather bleak odds of 7.9 to 1. When he says, "I desperately need a thirty-million-dollar jackpot—I really hope we don't get hit Wednesday," he means that the Texas Lottery needs to develop a much bigger lotto jackpot to attract a greater number of players and therefore greater revenue. And when Hosker says, "We're one of the few states that pays off for three out of six in lottery," you know GTECH isn't doing it out of the kindness of its heart. Instead, GTECH has discovered that a player who wins $3 by correctly guessing three out of six numbers typically spends his winnings in the next round of lotto, thus ensuring the lottery a built-in cash supply.

It is no wonder that GTECH commands a 75 percent share of the world's on-line lottery market, including 26 of the 35 American lottery states and countries such as Malaysia and Iceland. No company on the planet is more formidable at coaxing money from lottery players, nor more formidable at gaining access to them. In the course of obtaining lottery contracts, GTECH has been accused of bribing a California state senator, providing trips to elected officials in Oregon and Indiana, and placing convicted racketeers and gamblers on its payroll. (GTECH has vigorously denied any allegations of criminal wrongdoing.) GTECH brawled, says a rueful competitor, like street fighters to win the Texas contract.

Jim Hosker's bluntness is refreshing, but his is not the official voice of the Texas Lottery. That task falls to GSD&M, the Austin-based advertising firm that was awarded the $20 million lottery account and that, in effect, plays good cop to GTECH's bad cop. The Texas Lottery's admen have learned from the mistakes of others: The lottery's commercials have been almost rigorously low-key, avoiding the kind of hard-sell approach that has invited controversy in other states. "All along we determined to go out and market the lottery as wholesome and fun," says GSD&M's president, Roy Spence. "In the initial focus groups, we ran into the idea that Texans love to compete. So our feeling was that if we make the games fun, even if people don't win, they'll have a good time."

Spence's strategy concedes an arguable truth: The lottery is designed to take more money than it gives away. That, of course, is why Texas has a lottery. By legislative mandate, the lottery must return 35 percent of its sales to the state general revenue fund. Then there are administrative costs, fees to GTECH, and retailer incentives to factor in. By the time the state and the lottery operatives are given their cut, between 51 and 55 cents of every $1 has been spoken for. This leaves a pay-out rate of less than 50 percent, which is below the average rate of 51 percent in other states. By comparison, the average annual payout rate for horse racing in the U.S. is 81 percent, for all slot machines 89 percent, and for all casino craps games 98 percent. Lottery opponents delight in pointing out that the odds of winning a lotto jackpot are about as high as the odds of getting struck by lightning; indeed, statistically you are seven times more likely to be struck by lightning than to win the lottery. According to one researcher's profitability analysis, a player could spend $20 a week on the lotto for fifty years and still have no better than a one-in-two-hundred chance of winning a jackpot. Among all popular gambling activities, the Texas Lottery is literally the dumbest bet there is.

Still, the "fun" lies in the belief that a fellow could beat the odds and walk away with riches. What Spence calls a love of competition Jim Hosker calls something else. " They play out of greed," says the lottery veteran. "They play to win." Though bound by state policy not to "suggest that it is easy to win the largest prizes," the Texas Lottery brain trust subtly stokes the fantasy that victory is imminent. For every two million or so also-rans, there is a Doyle Norton for whom the state eagerly plays publicist. (After a Cambodian refugee won a lotto jackpot, comptroller Sharp announced, "None of us can truly comprehend the brutality of Tem Vuth's childhood in Cambodia. And very few of us will ever be able to really understand the fun and excitement of winning $12.6 million.") Our government now publishes a bi-monthly newsletter called the *Texas Lottery Winners' Gazette*, in which lotto winners reveal how they selected their lucky numbers and what they did with all that loot. One TV commercial shows the images of several lucky Texans within a circular frame, followed by the voice-over: "Play the game of Texas. Maybe we'll see *you* in the winner's circle!" A lottery claims office representative will happily oblige any request to recite the latest winning lotto combinations—not bothering to mention that this is a pointless exercise, since in a random drawing there is statistically no such thing as a hot number. Lottery press releases often point out that the latest big winner played numerous times before good fortune struck. The message is plain: If you're not winning, keep spending; your number is sure to come up.

All across the state, retailers—who get a 5-cent commission for every $1 ticket sold and one percent of every lottery jackpot if the winning ticket is purchased from their store—have joined hands with the government and GTECH to create a pep rally atmosphere, in which customers are exhorted to take a stab at instant prosperity. Numerous stores post photographs of winners on bulletin boards, adorn their walls with winning tickets, and offer "second-chance" drawings in which a losing ticket may qualify someone for a modest prize. Such tactics have been suggested by GTECH, which has seen all over the world what works and what doesn't. But a few inspired entrepreneurs have come up with ideas of their own. At Stateline Oil Company, 24 miles from Seminole and a few yards from the New Mexico border, Al Hester, Jr., offers a drive-through ticket booth; canopy-shaded picnic tables where ticket-scratchers can while away the hours; and a computer that selects previously unselected six-number lotto combinations. Hester is the state's top retailer by far, owing to the vanloads from Roswell and Carslbad who regularly venture across the border. (New Mexico has no lottery.) Hester's overall business is up by 670 percent since the lottery came to Texas. At times, the lottery players simply overwhelm the store, he says, "like ants coming out of the anthill."

The state's most relentlessly creative retailer is probably Melvin Joice, a Livingston horse breeder whose Melbo's Convenience Store is the top lottery outlet in East Texas. With his cowboy hat and his just-plain-sense twang, Joice comes off as equal parts Clayton Williams and Ross Perot. In anticipation of brisk sales, he built a large lottery room onto the back of his store—complete with a "Baptist door," so that his religious customers could sneak in and out. "If a jackpot winner buys his lotto ticket at my store," Joice says, "I will personally give him a five-thousand-dollar check just for buying it here. And I will personally pick him up in a limousine and personally drive him all the way to Austin to pick up his jackpot."

Joice does a booming business in instant tickets, and it's not hard to figure out why. "If you buy ten tickets from me," he declares, "I will give you this here free pen." Holding up the pen, which bears the store's logo, he continues: "Now, you can see that on the side of this pen there are three spots to scratch. If the pen I give you has the word 'five' three times underneath each of the three spots, I will give you another five instant tickets—free of charge."

In Dallas' top retail center, the Shop N Go on Central Expressway south, owner Pete Peterson orders his clerks to wish every ticket purchaser good luck. "A fish stinks from the head down," the round-faced, fast-talking boss philosophizes. "If I didn't like it, my help wouldn't like it. I've taught many a customer how to play lotto. I'll say, 'You might have an argument at the office about how the game is played, and I want you to be the one to win the argument. And while you're at it, take a few of these lotto slips and stick them in your glove compartment. Who knows? You might have a vision!'"

Peterson says lottery sales alone will bring him an extra $50,000 this year. But there's more to the joys of the lottery than just money, he insists. "It has changed the whole personality of the store," he says. "The three topics of conversation used to be the weather, the Cowboys, and local politics—and when people started talking politics, things could get pretty heated. But now you don't hear any complaining. It's like a ski lodge: Even the guy on crutches is smiling. They're happy losers."

After Stateline Oil Company, the state's second-biggest retailer is a Town and Country convenience store in McAllen, eight miles from the Mexican border. Owner Alvin Potter takes pride in his shop's status as a big-time revenue collector for the State of Texas. Chalkboards throughout the store list the latest hot numbers, urge customers to imagine what they would do with millions of dollars, and invoke a civic spirit: "This store is #2 in the state in Lotto sales and moving up on #1! Come on, McAllen!"

Potter is thrilled by all the business, but there's an element to it that perplexes him. "You know," he says slowly, "this is a poverty-stricken area. I've sold four million tickets, and it hasn't cut into my other business. Four million dollars! Where did it come from?"

An honest man, Potter does not try to convince anyone that all of his business is coming from the handful of Valley residents who are well off. But state officials have been less forthright. Early this spring, state lottery director Nora Linares released a summary of a demographic survey of Texas Lottery players. Noting that the survey results were somewhat inconclusive, the director nonetheless hammered home the good news in a cover letter for the report: "We were pleased to find, however, that those with the lowest levels of education and those with the smallest incomes are *least likely to play*. This is important to us—and should be reassuring to you—because of the widespread concern that the Lottery might 'victimize' those groups of people who are least prepared to understand the odds of winning or who can least afford to lose money playing the Lottery."

The survey results made front-page news throughout the state, and no one in the media openly questioned their accuracy. But a closer look at the survey reveals obvious flaws concerning which income groups play the lottery. To begin with, only Texans with telephones were surveyed. Of the 1,500 respondents, more than 20 percent refused to disclose their income, thus significantly reducing the population sample. Those who did reveal their income did not necessarily tell the truth. As Richard Murray, one of the two University of Houston political scientists who designed the survey, points out, "Low-income people tend to overstate their income, and there's no way to safeguard against that in the survey." But Murray and his co-researcher, Kent Tedin, say that the survey had a more severe flaw—namely, that they were asked to undertake it during an atypical period of lottery play. "Lotto had been in effect only nine or ten days when we began our study," says Tedin. "There had been only three or four lotto [drawings], and therefore there was absolutely no way of determining frequency of play. Instead, there was a big novelty factor, and a lot of people who played lotto then aren't likely to be playing now." The novelty factor, Murray says, caused "a big spike in the population sample." In short, everything about how and when the survey was taken skewed the results toward higher income levels.

There is additional evidence to contradict Linares' assertion that the lottery does not make much money off low-income groups. The survey summary acknowledges that most lottery players prefer the instant, or scratch-off, games over lotto, and further, that the largest percentage of instant players buy tickets several times a week. And who are these frequent buyers who provide the most significant percentage of lottery revenue? People in low-income groups. In a portion of the survey not included in the packet distributed to the press, Murray and Tedin reported, "Those with lesser incomes are more likely to play Scratch than those with higher incomes...Generally, those with lower incomes play more frequently."

In the end it doesn't take a sophisticated survey to prove that Ann Richards was right the first time: Texas Lottery revenue is coming largely from those who are not well off. Simply standing in one of the high-volume retail outlets and observing who the players are is evidence enough. For that matter, six of the state's top twenty retailers are Fiesta Marta in Houston, a chain that caters to a lower-middle-class customer base. (In contrast, Tom Thumb Grocery stores, which are located in comparatively more affluent neighborhoods, quit selling lottery tickets at the beginning of this year because their customers had lost interest in the games.)

State officials may not acknowledge who is playing the lottery, but the professionals at GTECH and Atlanta-based Dittler Brothers, the state's lottery-ticket printers, know. "An additional demographic characteristic which bodes well for ticket sales in Texas," said Dittler Brothers in its bid proposal, "is the substantial resident Hispanic population...While the lottery and its vendors must be careful not to approach this segment in a manner that would result in 'targeting' criticism, it will be an important part of the Texas player base and should be monitored closely..." Dittler Brothers helped suggest the Fiesta instant-ticket game, which the firm believed "should be popular with Hispanic segments of the player base." GTECH's proposal also targeted the Texas Hispanic population. The firm recommended that Texas inaugurate its lottery using 20,000 retail outlets—or 1 retailer for every 859 Texans—scattered throughout ten sales districts. The Houston sales district would average 1 retailer for every 908 consumers; the Dallas district, 1 for every 902. By far, the two most retailer-concentrated districts would be those districts containing the largest population of low-income Hispanics: McAllen with 1 retailer for every 576 consumers, and El Paso with 1 for every 495. The Texas Lottery followed GTECH's recommendations.

GTECH's Jim Hosker insists that it is "male yuppies" who play his games. "We market our product to people with discretionary incomes," he says. "If a lottery didn't do that, it would never make money." Indeed, no study has ever demonstrated that the poorest of the poor spend their last dollars on a game of chance. But the secret—known for years within the lottery industry and now revealed to Texas retailers such as McAllen's Alvin Potter—is that rich folks aren't the only ones with disposable income. The state comptroller's office has attempted to track the $1.8 billion in sales to determine where all that money came from. Early reports showed a slight drop in alcohol purchases and the expected slump in racetrack business. Otherwise, no state business appears to have suffered from the Texas Lottery. The genius of GTECH and the lottery officials is their ability to find almost $2 billion where no one thought to find it before: deep in the pockets of the working class.

One who remains unamused by GTECH's proficiency is Lieutenant Governor Bob Bullock. "I have two people in my office who have worked for me for many years, and I love them both dearly," he says. "Both of them spend two or three hundred dollars a month on the lottery. At twelve noon, when their lunch break comes, they head for the 7-Eleven down the street. And of course, they're broke as can be. I'm convinced they're as hooked on those tickets as I was on whiskey."

Deception 3. A Voluntary Tax

The ultimate line of defense for the lottery is that no one is forced to play it. Yet every veteran in the lottery industry knows that a lottery cannot succeed without constant promotion and a continued succession of games designed to keep the player interested and his wallet wide open. In its quest for revenue, the state is obliged to loosen the leash and let the industry entice the consumer any way it can. As lottery opponent David Hudson points out, "The state raises money from alcohol and tobacco taxes. But it doesn't get up every morning and beg people to buy a six-pack of beer so that we can raise revenue to educate the little children."

"If you want to play the lottery, great, and if you don't want to play, you shouldn't," says John Sharp. But the state comptroller's remark says more about himself than about the games over which he presides. Sharp voted no in the 1991 lottery referendum, and his reign since that time, however, skillful, has reflected his personal distaste for the concept. He has prevented GTECH from imposing sales quotas on retailers, rejected aggressive lottery advertisements, sent out GSD&M admen to keep an eye on the field activities of GTECH, denied retail permits to porn shops and to stores located near schools, and slowed the implementation of numerous games he found to be overly gimmicky. A case could be made that Sharp, by being such a spoilsport, has significantly diminished the lottery's earning potential. If we were going to have a lottery, shouldn't it be allowed to generate all the revenue it possibly can? Sharp considers the question while chomping on a cigar and studying his shoes. Then he says quietly, with a wry smile, "Not while I'm running it."

Sharp promised that the Texas Lottery would be run like a business. But businesses seek growth, and this particular business can grow only by getting more buyers and, especially, by getting buyers to buy more. Sharp has little stomach for this kind of market massaging. His immediate subordinate, however, has no such inhibitions: Nora Linares, the state lottery director, says she voted for the lottery in the 1991 referendum. "It's not like I'm pro-gambling. I felt it was the best way to balance the budget," she says. Linares believes that she provides a good balance to her less enthusiastic boss and adds, "Because he's as concerned about the lottery as he is, John tends to see things differently from the rest of us."

Though obviously bright and gregarious, Nora Linares possesses the same disingenuous streak one often finds in those politicians who have reconciled themselves to the lottery. She now says that she tends to agree with her demographic surveyors who say the study of lottery players is flawed; but this, of course, is long after she sent out numerous copies of the survey to the press and to politicians, accompanied by the cover letter in which she trumpeted the survey's proof that the lottery made relatively little money off of low-income groups.

"Unless you add on to your product mix, the players will get bored and you're just not going to be able to increase your revenues," says Linares. "So that's what we've been doing, and that's what we'll continue to do." The marketing drive in the Texas Lottery is like no other state-sponsored promotion. Almost every day the state lottery officials huddle with GTECH, Dittler Brothers, and GSD&M, and the underlying premise of each meeting is revenue enhancement. "It's been the most intensive business we've been in by far," says GSD&M's Roy Spence. "You can't just do a campaign and let it run. There's new games and educating the public about the new games—it's like a whole new campaign every six weeks."

Already in a year's time the push has been staggering. Twelve instant games have been introduced—almost double the amount the lottery had originally intended in the first year. Most of these games have been announced by Sharp or Linares at a well-staged press conference and accompanied by a promotional blitz. Beneath each game lies a meticulous strategy that serves the overall mission of maximizing revenues. The first two games, Lone Star Millions and Texas Match Up, offered especially unfavorable odds (1 in 7.90 and 1 in 6.81, respectively) and ungenerous payout rates (45.68 percent and 46.22 percent, respectively) because—as Dittler Brothers put it in its proposal—"at this juncture, low odds are not needed to spur sales." By the third game, Dittler Brothers predicted, sales would slump "because the instant product is no longer perceived to be fun and interesting and/or because the product is viewed as offering poor odds of winning…" Thus came Texas Two Step and its more favorable odds, made possible by eliminating the bigger prizes offered in the first two games.

For this game, and for each game that would follow, GSD&M used focus groups to probe the marketplace for soft spots. When lotto was introduced in November 1992, it was time, said the ticket printers, "to focus increased attention on the mid-tier prize levels…that reinforce the players' decision to play and encourage continued play." The new game, Stocking Stuffer, did precisely that by offering the highest payout rate (55.47 percent) up to that point.

The odds have differed on eleven out of the twelve games not because the state's level of generosity has varied but because lottery officials are continually tinkering with prize structures in an effort to get more people to play more often. In fact, when Linares introduced the tenth game, Fiesta, she declared, "The odds of winning are great," though the odds for Fiesta (1 in 4.93) were actually worse than the odds for the four games immediately preceding it (4.90, 4.67, 4.39, and 4.46, respectively). The two most recent instant games, Cactus Cash and Grand Slam, offer identical odds (1 in 4.87) but represent two different marketing ploys. Cactus Cash boasts the lottery's highest payout rate to date, 65 percent; this is being done, says Sharp, as "an experiment to see if higher payouts will attract more players" and thus increase revenues. Grand Slam is meant to cash in on baseball season, just as Stocking Stuffer and Touchdown were introduced as seasonal tie-ins. ("We tried to get one out for basketball season," says Linares, "but we didn't have time.") When the seasons change, so does the marketing strategy. The only ones who leave things to chance are the players.

Texans will soon be playing Quick Pick, a version of lotto in which a computer automatically selects a player's six numbers. Despite popular demand on the part of the public and the retailers, this industry staple took a full year to get to Texas. "I'm the guy who convinced them not to do Quick Pick," Jim Hosker says. "See, the customer has to decide he is responsible, not the computer, for whether or not he wins. If he keeps playing Quick Pick and losing, he'll say, 'This damn computer never gives me the good numbers!' And he'll quit playing. I've got to get the customer to think he's the reason he wins or loses."

Hosker's tactic has succeeded, says Linares. "People have bought into the game, they've learned it, and they have ownership with their numbers," she says. Still, Quick Pick is coming to Texas to keep the players in heat with another new gimmick, and following that, a "pick three" daily numbers game.

Looming in the distance is the VLT, or video lottery terminal, which has the rapid-motion action of a slot machine but not its far more favorable odds. South Dakota's revenue bonanza with VLTs has caught the attention of lottery directors around the country, including Linares, and video lottery firms have been roaming the state capitol seeking friends in high places. This legislative session, they nearly succeeded: A bill that would bring these devices to Texas made it out of a Senate committee, only to be returned to committee by order of Lieutenant Governor Bob Bullock, who demanded that legislators put the skids on their lottery fever. For now, the bill is dead. But Linares observes that most lottery states have VLTs and sees eventual passage of this measure as an inevitability.

"We've had cocaine, now let's go for crack," says the Christian Life Commission's Weston Ware in disgust. "That's what a video lottery is." Ware's analogy is apt, however extreme it might be. For in the lottery, our elected officials have found a politically cheap revenue panacea, a tax that—for them, if for no one else—is utterly painless. By passing the lottery referendum, Texas voters have unwittingly given the Legislature permission to pummel them with get-rich-quick schemes, to which they will submit "voluntarily," in the name of fun and greed. The ends to which we will be barraged are limited only by the imagination of the lottery industry. In time, the statehouse's growing hunger for revenues may compromise the requirement that the Texas Lottery avoid enticing ads. Missouri has already tossed out its legislated lottery advertising requirements in a hell-bent quest for revenue.

In a year's time the Texas Lottery has created a statewide spectacle and provided cheap entertainment for many. Of the 11 million who have played the games, a few dozen have become millionaires. But for the state as a whole, the lottery is a loser. At best, it has helped to compensate for state budgetary shortfalls, but at what price? Scratch beneath the surface of a lottery ticket and what you find is a plainly regressive tax, elicited with such force of money and energy that the term "voluntary" is stripped of its essence. A year from now, as the public relations luster of the lottery dims, it will become even more apparent that the lottery is not the answer for underfunded education, overcrowded prisons, and a host of other social ills. But by then, Texans will be fully accustomed to having their pockets picked. The state has already bought its ticket.

At the press conference immediately following his million-dollar drawing, Doyle Norton sat stupefied amid a knot of microphones and cameras. Had he felt lucky when he awakened that morning? "A little. I had a feeling..." Did he know what he was going to do with the money? "I don't know...Put it in the bank, I guess." Was he thrilled beyond words? "It's hard to say. The whole thing feels like a dream." The other, lesser winners sat nearby, grinning relaxed smiles. For the six of them, the drawing had been a blast. For Norton, however, the "fun and excitement of winning" had yet to register on his face.

A question was put to the 24-year-old lawn-service man: "Will you keep playing the lottery?" And at this, Doyle Norton seemed to snap out of his dream. "Oh, I don't think so," he said, smiling at last. "I think I've made enough money."

The lottery had lost a customer, but back in Austin, no one at the GTECH and state lottery offices was crying. Norton had flung the hat for the cameras; he had done his part. In the meantime, the number on Jim Hosker's and Nora Linares' computer monitors kept growing.

A Little Scratch

We bought five hundred tickets. Here's what happened.

We all know that the odds of winning a fortune playing the lottery are remote. In the latest instant games, for example, we were told that the chance of scratching off a $1,000 ticket is 1 in 60,000. On the other hand, assuming that every ticket printed is sold, someone has got to come away lucky. So how difficult is it, really, to beat the odds?

Texas Monthly decided to find out. On April 22 we wagered $500 on the lottery by purchasing from an Austin vendor one packet each of the two new instant games created by the Texas Lottery: Grand Slam and Cactus Cash. Each packet contained 250 $1 tickets.

Grand Slam pits the player against an opposing team. The ticket features three boxes to scratch: your score, your opponent's score, and the prize you'll win if your score exceeds that of your opponent. On each ticket, you play two such games; thus, as it reads on the tickets, you have "two chances to win!" This is a popular gimmick in the lottery industry, since players perceive that the second game gives them a better shot at winning. In reality, however, no ticket has two winning games; the odds are the same as they would be if there were only one game per ticket. Overall, when playing Grand Slam, you stand a 1-in-4.87 chance of winning something. "Something" usually means $1 or $2, as the odds of winning either of these are 1 in 12—exactly five thousand times greater than the odds of winning the top prize, $1,000.

Of course, we did as all gamblers do: We ignored the odds. The way we figured it, out of our 250 tickets, all we needed to break even were two $100 winners (odds of winning one: 1 in 2,824), one $40 (1 in 1,200), and one $10 (1 in 250). And of course, a single $1,000 ticket and we would be sipping Dom Perignon. So a dozen or so of us scratched away. Those who played only to win scratched the scores and didn't bother with the prize box if they lost. Those who wished to savor the drama scratched the prize box first, then the opponent's score, and finally, with bated breath, the box that would determine glorious victory or another buck down the drain.

By the end, 23 of the 250 tickets were $1 winners, 19 won us $2, 3 got us $4, 4 earned $5, and 1 paid out $20. Nobody scratched a $10, $40, $100, or $1,000 ticket. Of the 250 Grand Slam tickets, 50 were winners, meaning we conquered the overall odds by a favor of .13—so we spent $250 and got back $113.

"Okay, so we're down $137," we told ourselves. "No problem." We still had a packet of 250 Cactus Cash tickets. And these, we figured, would do us better since, according to the lottery director's press release, this particular game "returns 65 percent of ticket sales back into prizes for Lottery players— more than any other instant-win ticket." However, the same press release states that the overall odds of winning at Cactus Cash are 1 in 4.87, identical to the odds for Grand Slam, which pays out only 55 percent of its sales in prizes. The difference is that Cactus Cash has roughly twice as many $5, $10, and $20 tickets— "mid-tier winners," in industry parlance—as Grand Slam. This means, for example, that the odds of scratching off a $20 winner are 1 in 250 for Cactus Cash, as opposed to 1 in 500 for Grand Slam.

Cactus Cash is a tic-tac-toe game; scratch off three cacti in a row, and you win whatever is indicated in the prize box. Unlike Grand Slam, you don't get "two chances to win." But the lottery uses a different technique in this game to excite players: the "heartstopper." If you scratch three in a row, you've won, but if you scratch two, well, you've almost won. As it turns out, in Cactus Cash you'll never buy a ticket that doesn't have at least two in a row; you've either got a victory or a near victory. Each ticket provides either a winning experience or a heartstopper;

thus each ticket, according to the conventional wisdom of the lottery industry, encourages further play.

Yet the results were again discouraging. As with Grand Slam, only 50 of our 250 tickets were winners. Not only did we practically match the overall odds of 1 in 4.87, but we won almost as many of each denomination as the individual odds predicted we would: 1 out of 12.5 $1 tickets (against the stated odds of 1 in 12), 1 out of 15.6 $2 tickets (1 in 16), 1 out of 41.7 $4 tickets (1 in 42), and so on. We actually beat the payout rate by recouping 70 percent of our investment, but it was small consolation: We spent $250 and won only $176 of it back.

If only the heartstoppers had been the real thing. We tabulated that if the near victories had counted, we would have won a truly heartstopping $56,887. This awfully high figure prompted us to take a closer look at the losing tickets. It turned out that while our winning tickets never turned out to be worth $100 or $1,000, 99 of the 200 losing heartstoppers tickets happened to be of those denominations. In contrast, our 250 tickets actually featured more winning $1 and $2 tickets than losing $1 and $2 tickets. Using lottery industry logic, this makes perfect sense. After all, is a $2 almost-winner going to stop your heart? But the real cunning lies in the frequent appearance of the $1,000 almost-winner. Extrapolating from our experiences—and considering how closely our winners matched the stated odds, we feel this is a safe leap—the odds of scratching a $1,000 heartstopper are a stunning 1 in 4.9. Put this in perspective. The unlikeliest thing that can happen to you while playing Cactus Cash is the 1-in-60,000 chance of winning $1,000. Yet the *most* likely thing you'll encounter is a ticket that says you came only one cactus away from winning a thousand bucks. Every fifth ticket, you'll come just that close—meaning all you need to do is repeat this five-ticket purchasing cycle 12,000 times, and odds are you'll see that winning $1,000 ticket.

Best of luck, since we're quitting while we're not completely bustola. To our surprise, though perhaps not to the lottery's, *Texas Monthly* played the odds, virtually matched them—and walked away $211 lighter.

Ask Dr. Lotto

Everything You Should Know About the "Game of Texas."

When you buy a lottery ticket, where does your dollar go?

Currently, 45 cents goes into the prize pool. At the end of August, however, this amount will rise to 55 cents. The share that goes into the state treasury to help fund the state budget will drop from 35 cents to 30 cents. The hope is that larger prizes will attract more ticket buyers. The remaining 15 cents will be divided among the comptroller's office, for administrative costs (5 cents); the retailers, as commission for selling tickets (5 cents); GTECH, for operating the lottery (4 cents); and retailers who sell a winning lotto ticket (1 cent).

What does the state do with its money?

It goes into the general revenue fund, which can be spent on anything in the state budget. Well over half of the general revenue fund is spent on health and human services, education, and prisons.

Why doesn't all the revenue go to education, as is widely perceived?

In 1991 the Legislature decided against dedicating all net lottery proceeds to the state education budget, and it defeated a similar provision this session. But the idea keeps resurfacing. Opponents say that the public schools should not have to depend on such an uncertain source of funding. They point to California, where a decline in lottery revenues during the late eighties resulted in cuts in the education budget. Still, roughly half of the states with lotteries continue to dedicate some or all of their lottery dollars to a variety of causes: to senior citizens in Pennsylvania, to transportation in Arizona, to the arts in Massachusetts, and to water conservation projects in Colorado.

How do you get the money you win playing the instant games?

If you scratch an instant ticket and your prize is less than $600, you can cash in your ticket at any lottery retailer. At least you're supposed to be able to. A number of retailers have shown a reluctance to pay out awards of $100 and up. In any event, a prize greater than $599 must be redeemed at 1 of the 24 claim offices scattered throughout the state. Still, there's no guarantee you'll get everything that you've won. Before the state hands over the money it runs a computer check to see if the winner is delinquent in child-support payments or owes state taxes or student loans. Whatever is owed is deducted from the winnings.

How do you win at lotto?

Correctly guess three of the six numbers and you win $3. If you guess four or five out of the six, your winnings can range from less than $100 to several thousand dollars, depending on the size of the jackpot and the number of other winners. The players who get all six numbers right split the jackpot, which thus far has ranged from $2 million to $50 million.

Does this mean that millions of dollars are sitting in the state treasury waiting to be won?

No. Here's how it works: After a lotto drawing for a jackpot worth, say, $4 million fails to produce any winners, lottery officials determine the roll-over—that is, how much the pot will be increased for the next drawing. The bigger the jackpot, the greater the sales; so the incentive is great to jack up the $4 million pot to something like $8 million. But before any decision is reached, the officials estimate how much ticket revenue the higher jackpot will produce and factor in the cost of purchasing $8 million in heavily discounted U.S. Treasury bonds structured for twenty annual payments. Only after these steps are taken is the size of the new jackpot announced. If the next lotto drawing still finds no winners, the process is repeated. If, however, someone correctly guesses the six numbers, then that person receives twenty annual payments of $288,000 ($400,000 less 28 percent deducted for income taxes); in effect, the jackpot is an annuity worth $8 million. The procedure means that winners get their money, but not all at once, and they can't invest the lump sum.

If a lotto jackpot winner dies, does the state reclaim the prize?

No. "The annuity is a zero coupon bond," says comptroller John Sharp, "and like any other piece of property, you can will it to whomever you want." He adds wearily, "I get asked that question everywhere I go." R.D.

Part IV

Corruption, Lawbreaking and the Mob

Just Like Old Times

One of the most cited reasons for supporting legalized gambling is that it keeps the business out of the hands of crooks. But that logic simply doesn't hold up. Though casinos are no longer controlled outright by mobsters, wiseguys still have their fingers in the pie when it comes to providing services like security and paper. In fact, when the chief of the FBI's organized crime section was asked a few years back which crime families were interested in Indian casinos, for example, he answered, "I don't know any that aren't."

Aside from ongoing mob relations, legalized gambling brings about its own brand of corruption and criminal activity; with so much money changing hands, politicians and business interests are bound to get a little greedy. According to a 1996 opinion piece in the *Des Moines Register*: "As competition within the gambling industry grows, so does the need for support in the public sector. This need has led to serious corruption. In Arizona in 1990, six legislators pleaded guilty to accepting bribes and illegal campaign contributions to legalize casino gambling. In Kentucky in 1992, seven legislators pleaded guilty to accepting bribes from lobbyists representing gaming interests. In West Virginia in 1990, former Gov. Arch Moore Jr. pleaded guilty to accepting a bribe from gaming interests. And the list goes on and on...When money becomes the motivation for public policy, the community loses." In November 1996, according to the Minneapolis *Star Tribune*, the most prominent American Indian leader in Minnesota, Darrell "Chip" Wadena, was sentenced to four years in prison for crimes related to his tribe's casino gambling business. Among other misdeeds, he was found to have taken a bribe from a contractor who helped build the Shooting Star Casino in Mahnomen.

Some argue that legalized gambling actually expands the market for illegal gambling. "The FBI estimates that a hefty $40 billion is bet illegally per year," says a January 1995 Focus on the Family report by Ronald A. Reno entitled "You Bet Your Life." "[Author and professor Robert] Goodman and others contend that there is a simple explanation for this: By enlarging the pool of bettors and, at the same time, reducing gambling's stigma, the state actually creates an increased market for illegal gambling activities. The federal government's commission on gambling, in its 1976 report, found this to be true. It pointed out that nearly one-quarter of those who participate in legal commercial gambling also engage in illegal gambling. In addition, the commission found that the illegal gambling rate jumped from 9 percent in states with no legalized gambling to 22 percent in states where three forms of gambling were permitted." Though the image is cleaner, the underside of gambling looks remarkably like it did in the good old days.

GTECH

They're In It to Win It

Lottery Giant GTECH's
Controversial Rise to Power

John Riley with Stephanie Saul
December 6, 1995
Newsday, Inc. Copyright © 1995
From the Series "Gambling: The New National Pastime"

Minneapolis—On the floor of the North American Association of State and Provincial Lotteries trade show here in October, you could order a latte at the GTECH Espresso Cafe. Or you could step inside the GTECH Player's Corner and grab a Tropikeno Cooler or a Quick Draw Margarita, named in honor of the wildly successful new keno game GTECH Corporation just introduced in New York.

You could sit at the bar and watch the bouncing keno ball pick numbers every five minutes on six television screens. Just like it bounces on thousands of screens in bars and taverns in New York. And you could read about the $10 million a week New Yorkers were betting in a flashy brochure that promises to tell "how Club Keno can mean big numbers for your lottery!"

Or, if you wanted some tips on how to make it come true for your state, you could wander up to the seminar on legislative lobbying and listen to GTECH official Gene Mansfield summarize the state of the industry for a roomful of lottery officials. "We're all salespersons in this room," Mansfield reminded the group. "You sell tickets. We sell products. Selling the legislatures is all of our jobs."

In an industry in which annual U.S. sales have exploded to more than $34 billion, nobody does it better than GTECH. And nobody has made more headlines doing it, either.

The story of GTECH's rise to a position where it controls 26 of 37 lottery contracts in the United States shows how a company can prosper from the nation's increasing use of lotteries to provide state revenues. And it's a story that has been accompanied by an increasing reputation for political as well as technical skill, headlines in state after state over its lobbying and other aggressive tactics to get and keep contracts, and criminal charges against its former chief salesman.

Few of the Rhode Island lottery giant's customers are bigger than New York, where GTECH controls separate contracts for managing both instant ticket sales and online games. Under those contracts, GTECH leases to the state central computer equipment and vendor terminals, operates the online games, distributes instant tickets, collects the money and provides a range of technical advice and marketing information. It gets between one and two pennies out of every dollar from the state's $3-billion-plus in lottery sales—and has now added its rapid-play keno game to the state's table of products.

But in New York as elsewhere, GTECH's activities have been fraught with controversy. The firm originally got a foothold here in the late 1980s, when lottery director John Quinn awarded it half of the online contract. GTECH hired Quinn nine months later. In 1992, while it was bidding for the full contract, it retained Gov. Mario Cuomo's former patronage secretary as its lobbyist—only to accept his resignation after the relationship was publicized.

This year, a team of GTECH lobbyists and Gov. George Pataki—who grew up in Peekskill with GTECH chairman Guy Snowden—persuaded the legislature to approve Quick Draw keno. Then, in closed door negotiations, the company won pricing concessions that could add millions of dollars a year to the financial bonanza GTECH will reap from keno in return for increasing the size of the state's online network by 2,500 terminals.

Altogether, internal lottery documents examined by *Newsday* show, the company's contract—estimated to be worth $152 million before it was awarded in 1993—is now expected to bring in more than $258 million over six years. GTECH's excess revenues over its costs are estimated in state documents at $73.1 million—or 28.29 percent of gross revenues, compared to 22.2 percent on GTECH's average lottery service contract.

Inside the state, such figures provide grist for critics. "GTECH is making out like a bandit in this," complains Sen. Frank Padavan (R-Queens), an opponent of the Quick Draw game. And outside observers say GTECH's history here reflects a worrisome trend of companies bidding low to get contracts, and then involving themselves in lobbying and politics to try to enhance the value of the deal by winning approval for new games.

"It's sensitive, it's troubling and it's something that each lottery director must deal with in a way they feel comfortable," says Michael Jones, a Chicago lottery consultant who headed the Illinois lottery in the 1980s. "It does suggest that you're allowing political power to be exercised by someone whose relationship with the state is only as a winning bidder."

The lottery, for its part, defends its contract with GTECH, and a spokeswoman for Pataki said he had nothing to do with recent changes. "This was done by the head of the lottery division," said press secretary Zenia Mucha.

GTECH says that its role in New York has been completely above-board, that the contract amendment was justified by New York's need to get new terminals for Quick Draw up and running quickly, and that any attempt to compare the profitability of New York to other contracts is like comparing apples to oranges. "It's much the same as trying to compare average costs for heating your home in Arizona to heating your home in New York," said GTECH spokesman Bob Rendine.

And more broadly, Rendine blames criticism of GTECH's lobbying and efforts to wield political influence on smear tactics by the competition, and he points out that the company has never been found to have engaged in wrongdoing by any official inquiry. "Without the perpetuation of these stories by irresponsible members of the media, there would be none of this," Rendine said. "Frankly, it doesn't bother or affect any of our customers."

One example: While GTECH was a major campaign contributor in the past—giving as much as $300,000 in one year, according to the *Chicago Tribune*—it gave up the practice of making corporate campaign contributions more than two years ago, Rendine says. The company now requires officers to clear contributions through an internal committee and prohibits lobbyists from making contributions on its behalf. "We've tried very hard to end that practice," he says. "...But that doesn't keep people from talking about it."

GTECH did, according to reports compiled by Common Cause, make $55,000 in federal "soft money" contributions to the Republican Party organization in the first six months of this year, and a similar amount in the 1993-94 election cycle. Rendine says the new policy applies only to contributions to individual candidates. As to the reports of $300,000 annually prior to adoption of the new policy, Rendine refuses to confirm or deny it but says it is "minuscule" compared to what other large companies give.

In part, experts say, the controversy that follows GTECH reflects the winner-take-all nature of the lottery business. Contracts to run a state's lottery generally run for five or six years, with an option to extend for a similar period. That means that in every state, and especially the big ones like New York, the prize of multi-millions in revenues is available only once every five or ten years. With the stakes so high, GTECH and its rivals have had good reason for a hard-nosed approach—and have used tactics that differ, if at all, only in degree.

"The expertise that's required and the capital investment are fairly significant," says Jeff Perlee, a former counsel for the GTECH-run Illinois lottery who was selected by Pataki as New York's new lottery director earlier this year. "It reduces the number of potential companies. The ones that are out there are fiercely competitive. They'll knock each other over the head."

That being said, GTECH has—more often than not—been the one left standing. Snowden, a computer expert, and Victor Markowicz, a mathematician, founded the company in 1981 after purchasing the lottery division of Datatrol, their employer, for $4.3 million. They inherited only a few clients, but saw the potential for growth in the application of computer technology to states' appetite for non-tax revenues.

By the late 1980s, there were five companies pursuing online contracts. But an amazing string of successes between 1989 and 1994 left GTECH in a dominant position with 26 contracts. Its major rival, Automatic Wagering International, has eight.

Overall, in its last fiscal year, GTECH sported gross profits of $235 million—results that have made it a Wall Street darling and its co-founders, Snowden and Markowicz, millionaires many times over. According to Securities and Exchange Commission filings, each received more than $2.8 million in compensation in 1995, and as of May 1 each controlled about 1.57 million shares of GTECH stock—currently trading at $28 a share.

One reason for the company's success, experts say, has been its technical skill, research and development, and capable performance. "We believe GTECH is simply the best at what they do," says Perlee. GTECH's Rendine, likewise, says the firm's "excellent quality products" and "cost-effective prices and heavy research and development investment" are the main reasons for its success.

But the company's other activities—lobbying, political giving, cultivating close relationships with lottery directors—have also drawn notice and raised concerns about how the rivalry for contracts is affecting public perceptions of lotteries. Referring to GTECH's lobbying and political activities, Perlee said, "It may be unnecessary and may create unfounded suspicions." "They're dealing with politicians directly, they donate, they pressure the legislature," says William Thompson, a professor of public administration at the University of Nevada-Las Vegas who studies gambling. "That gives it a dirty tinge, that gloss of dirty money."

Among other arenas, GTECH's activities have come under scrutiny in federal criminal cases filed against its former chief salesman, J. David Smith, in Kentucky and New Jersey. In the

Kentucky case, Smith and Rogers Wells—a well-connected former state official—were charged with defrauding GTECH through a scheme in which Smith approved phony invoices and Wells kicked back some of the money he received to Smith.

But the defense, at trial earlier this year, argued that the payments were authorized by GTECH as part of a larger pattern of giving money for no work to more than a dozen companies in various states to buy "good will" for GTECH.

Those payments, noted Smith lawyer Dominic Amorosa in a recent interview, were at least at times designed for political benefits. "Good will being important to GTECH in terms of making things flow more smoothly than they would otherwise flow," he said, "...you definitely want the word spread that GTECH is OK. You definitely want the word spread and it isn't bad to have it spread in the upper echelons of government."

GTECH chairman Snowden asserted his Fifth Amendment privilege against testifying before a grand jury (Rendine says it was because he didn't have time to prepare), and the judge ultimately dismissed the case with a finding that prosecutors had failed to prove that GTECH didn't authorize the payments. A companion case, in New Jersey, is scheduled to go to trial next year.

In that case, Smith and two men with ties to officials in the administration of Gov. James Florio were charged with a scheme in which Smith arranged for the men to get $739,000 from GTECH to use their influence to obtain approval for a keno game, and the men kicked back $157,000 to Smith. One of the men—Joseph LaPorta—was a relative of Florio's chief of staff, and he has told FBI agents that the introduction to Smith and GTECH came through Roger Stone, a veteran Republican political operative who has lobbied for GTECH for years.

According to court records, LaPorta told the FBI that, in one meeting with Stone, LaPorta noted that he was a Democrat and Stone was a prominent Republican. "Which team are you on?" LaPorta asked Stone. Stone's response: "I'm on the green team." Stone no longer represents GTECH, according to the company.

Stone, in an interview, denied LaPorta's account. "I categorically deny the comments attributed to me," Stone said. "They were an attempt to implicate me falsely in this matter and I have cooperated fully with the government."

GTECH itself was not accused of wrongdoing in either case, and was—Rendine points out—the alleged victim of kickback schemes. But the cases, at the least, have been an embarrassment to the company. Although it has described defense allegations of "goodwill payments" as a "gross exaggeration," GTECH has canceled some contracts in which no or inadequate services were being provided after a review prompted by the Kentucky trial, Rendine says. And they are far from the only controversies the company has been caught up in.

•In Maryland, in 1991, GTECH's lobbying team included disgraced former Gov. Marvin Mandel. As part of its bid for the state lottery contract, it promised subcontracts to businesses controlled by politically well-connected individuals, including a former numbers operator who had ties to Gov. William Schaefer and won a printing contract from GTECH. After an investigation spawned by news reports that GTECH's lead lobbyist had inside information about the bidding, the lobbyist was indicted on unrelated charges involving a scheme to launder campaign contributions.

No wrongdoing relating to GTECH was found in the criminal inquiry, and GTECH has described the hiring of Mandel as a mistake. Rendine says the former numbers operator was not offered a subcontract to gain influence. "I don't think who you hire as a printer has any influence over anything at all except the quality of your printing," the spokesman said.

•In Arizona, in 1993, after the state's lottery director insisted that GTECH comply with costly contract provisions requiring it to add instant-ticket validators to online terminals, director Bruce Mayberry says he received a rotting leg of mutton in the mail from top salesman Smith. "Enjoy," said a note inside. Later, Mayberry says, a GTECH lobbyist with close ties to Gov. Fyfe Symington successfully pushed for his ouster. "GTECH's motive is always to own the lottery director," said

Mayberry, who now works for AWI, in an interview. "If they can't, they try to get the lottery director fired."

Rendine's response: "That's moronic." He says the whole controversy was instigated by AWI. An investigation by the Arizona attorney general found that the mutton was sent to Mayberry "without sinister intent," and "did not develop evidence" to prove Mayberry was inappropriately terminated.

•In California, a lobbyist for GTECH and a number of other companies—Clayton Jackson—was charged with bribing a state senator on various matters, including a bill opposed by GTECH. The legislator pleaded guilty to racketeering based on that and other corrupt acts, and the lobbyist was convicted of racketeering, though the jury did not find Jackson guilty on the counts relating to GTECH. Also, a top aide to Gov. Pete Wilson, after picking former Illinois lottery director Sharon Sharp to head California's lottery, then went to work as a GTECH lobbyist. Sharp, later criticized for structuring bidding for a new lottery contract in a way that favored GTECH, resigned after tapes of Jones referring to her as "our gal" surfaced.

The procurement was ultimately reviewed and approved by a state panel. Rendine says GTECH and other clients were unaware of Jackson's activities, and says, "we have no idea" why he referred to Sharp as "our gal."

•In Florida, where GTECH and its chief competitor, AWI, are locked in a bitter battle for a new contract, the two combined have hired an estimated 12 lobbyists, according to GTECH lobbyist Barry Hornbein. GTECH also hired—for a non-lobbying post, according to Rendine—a former deputy director of the lottery who resigned just before the bidding began. GTECH has also charged the existing lottery director, Marcia Mann, with bias and pushed for her removal. "It's guerrilla warfare," says one lobbyist.

To those in the middle, the Florida battle has become all too typical of lottery wars between AWI and GTECH played out in state after state. "If you start to look at the allegations that have been made one to another, I don't think any state would like to have either one," says Rep. Jim King, a

Jacksonville Republican on the legislative committee oversee-
ing the lottery. "The industry has been characterized by FBI
investigations, political malfeasance…allegations of bribery
and basketfuls of allegations of corruptness."

•In New York, GTECH got a foothold in 1987, after lottery
directory Quinn decided to split a contract previously held by
Control Data Corp. and gave half to GTECH. In 1988, Quinn quit
and went to work for GTECH as its director of Far East operations.

Subsequent audits by the state comptroller criticized the
division of the contract and noted that GTECH was getting
2.27 percent of sales, while CDC was getting only 1.36. GTECH
says Quinn's decision to split the contract was unrelated to his
subsequent hiring, and that it won half of the contract because
it was one of the two low bidders.

The next battle came in 1991 and 1992, when GTECH
and CDC competed for a consolidated five-year contract.
GTECH had a marginal cost advantage—1.525 percent of sales
under $2.5 billion and .66 percent over, compared to a CDC
matrix of 1.539 percent and .45 percent. But an evaluation
committee scored CDC's proposal higher based on technical
merit, and stuck with that view after lottery director Peter
Lynch asked for a review.

Lynch, however, continued to delay making the award.
Behind the scenes, he had asked for a state police investigation
of both bidders. And GTECH hired Tonio Burgos, Gov. Mario
Cuomo's former patronage secretary, to a lucrative lobbying
contract—only to request his resignation after the lobbying
deal came to light.

Amid those machinations, CDC sold its lottery division to
a Montana company—Video Lottery Technologies, which
began operating the unit under the AWI name—and Lynch
requested a review of the impact of the sale on the bids. The
evaluation committee still scored the CDC/VLT bid higher,
while expressing concerns about its financial future, and draft-
ed two identical memoranda on May 15, 1992, that differed
only in their conclusions. They signed the one recommending
GTECH, and Lynch followed that recommendation.

As things have turned out, GTECH's New York contract has proven more lucrative than might have been anticipated. During the bidding, Lynch had asked both competitors to be prepared to offer a rapid-action keno game as part of their bids. But the lottery division didn't take keno into account when scoring the bids—assuming, instead, an average of $2 billion in annual sales over the term of the contract, and no trigger of the $2.5 billion breakpoint at which CDC's price proposal became lower than GTECH's.

By the time the contract was signed in February, 1993, however, lottery officials had both decided to expand the contract from five years to six years and had negotiated a separate appendix on keno. While providing a fast-draw keno game was included in the initial bid, it turned out, the hardware to make it operate effectively was not.

On top of GTECH's basic percentage, the appendix said, GTECH would get $15,000 a week for random-number-generating equipment—or $780,000 a year. It also negotiated to get $12.50 a week for video terminals and other equipment needed to offer the game. Internal lottery documents indicate that the monitors will cost GTECH $5.4 million and produce revenues of $9.5 million until the contract expires in February, 1999.

In the end, it took three years for fast-draw keno to finally win legislative approval after it was first proposed by Gov. Mario Cuomo as part of his budget. But it finally won passage this year with Pataki's support and lobbying by a six-member team organized by GTECH. The contract, in the wake of the Burgos episode, had prohibited GTECH from using lobbyists in New York without permission. Lottery officials say they finally granted permission—while Lynch was still director—because the executive branch of New York's government needed GTECH's help to combat "misinformation" circulated by opponents.

With the lottery projecting more than $300 million in keno sales this year, and more than $700 million next year, the new game promised to be a bonanza for GTECH. But after helping win approval for keno, GTECH took a tough stance with lottery officials in negotiations over the enhancements needed to meet the ambitious revenue projections—special "annunciator boards" to display the game in spacious locations, self-service terminals for players, and an expansion of the state's online network from 10,000 to 12,500 terminals.

The final deal called on GTECH to provide between 500 and 7,500 "annunciator boards" at an additional $15 per week per location. The lottery also ordered between 3,500 and 7,500 self-service terminals at $10.50 per week per location. Internal lottery documents indicate that GTECH's costs on the two items will be about $6.7 million, and its projected revenues about $11.9 million.

The biggest item was the additional terminals. For those, the lottery agreed to permit GTECH to earn its higher contract rate of 1.525 percent on up to $1 billion in new keno sales, on top of the $2.5 billion breakpoint for other online games at which GTECH's rate was supposed to drop under the original contract. Online sales were at $2.3 billion last year, and keno sales—if counted against the original breakpoint—would likely have pushed GTECH into its lower rate range. The potential benefit to GTECH from getting a higher percentage on an additional $1 billion in sales could be millions of dollars a year during the last three years of its contract.

Perlee, who signed off on the final amendment, acknowledges that GTECH is doing handsomely in New York—but says it's a "corollary" to the lottery's success. He insists that the price adjustment he agreed to actually reduced the windfall GTECH might have received if keno had been installed on the existing 10,000 terminal network.

And, he says, the final deal reflected the fact that budget demands gave the lottery little time to seek competitive bids, noting that "...the imperative to get terminals to achieve the revenue threshold put the lottery in a relatively weak negotiating position."

GTECH, for its part, makes no apologies. "Obviously, no one should fault the company for negotiating in good faith with a customer," Rendine says. "We're a public business and not a non-profit business. I think that should be understandable. Were we not to receive payment for services rendered, we would not be a business."

Cardrooms
A Draw for Criminals

Police, FBI, Legislature
Keep Close Watch on Casino Growth

David Dietz
San Francisco Chronicle, August 19, 1996

To someone crossing his path, Khiem Pham was just a struggling businessman who ran a small Vietnamese cafe, drove an aging Hyundai hatchback and lived modestly with family and friends on a leafy street in south San Jose.

But Pham was anything but run-of-the-mill in 1993 to authorities. They tapped his phone, spied on him with undercover agents, staked out his green stucco house, followed him wherever he went—and finally arrested him and 13 others on cocaine trafficking charges.

Court files show, however, that the law had a front-row seat to far more than drug deals. Although the case was narrowed for prosecution reasons, records of an FBI-led investigation show a graphic picture of how Pham and an organized crime ring allegedly built a robust loansharking and drug business—all on the floor of the Garden City Casino in San Jose.

The FBI's allegations that Pham used a cardroom as a criminal launching pad provide a singular example of why police in some California cities see the gambling operations as breeding centers for offenses ranging from home-invasion robberies to money laundering.

In their investigation of Pham, authorities worked their way inside a Hong Kong-based gang that allegedly preyed for at least a year on struggling gamblers, including card dealers, and muscled the victims when they fell behind on stratospheric loan payments. "If the loan victim doesn't pay," FBI agent Gary

Burton said in a court document, "then [Pham's] underlings will cut the victim's arms or legs as punishment."

As the cardroom industry grows in California, crime is raised as a powerful issue. Using it as a prime weapon, casino opponents from South San Francisco to Pomona succeeded last year in defeating proposals to establish cardrooms in their communities.

In Sacramento, crime is a key prod in legislative efforts to impose tighter controls on casinos. In San Jose, where two of the busiest casinos in California are located, police have been particularly vocal about crime and have stood in the way of casino expansion efforts without safeguards.

For years, cardrooms were mostly small, dreary places that didn't cause much of a stir. But the industry surged in the last decade, fed by high-stakes gambling that came in tandem with California's boom in Asian immigrants.

Where cardrooms once were marked by sleepy play, it is not uncommon today to enter one of California's glitzy new gambling palaces and find patrons vying in Asian games with thousands of dollars in chips in front of them.

In 1994, cardroom revenues jumped 134 percent, to $706 million, according to the state attorney general's office. The total wagered in casinos: about $8.5 billion—four times what the state lottery took in.

With that kind of money sloshing around, police say, it's little wonder that the crooks are circling.

"The very nature of the business is going to attract a lot of slimeballs," says Sergeant Randy Spitze, head of a four-member San Jose police vice team that watches the casinos. "If they think there's a lot of easy money, you are going to have them hanging around."

The lure of casinos is particularly strong to organized crime, which has even sought to muscle its way into club management, law officers say. Two years ago, members of a gang known as Red Fire shot at a card club executive in the East Bay in an apparent power struggle.

"Throughout California, organized crime has continued to make a strong effort to infiltrated the gaming industry," says San

Jose Police Chief Louis Cobarruviaz. "These efforts are prompted by the tremendous cash flow and skimming that such cardrooms present."

In Pham's case, court files portrayed a gang with Far East roots and an extensive loan-sharking, drug-running and illegal betting operation in California. Garden City was a key target, but court files show that the ring also operated in two other Bay Area casinos—Artichoke Joe's in San Bruno and the Oaks Club in Emeryville.

Inside Garden City, an A-frame building that anchors a small shopping center, Pham, 30, and his associates routinely sold cocaine smuggled from Mexico and played bankers of sorts to down-and-out gamblers, records showed.

For loans ranging from $5,000 to $40,000, the ring charged interest rates of up to 10 percent a week.

At first, the files said, the gang made loans without collateral and threatened the victims—sometimes inside the clubs—when payments lapsed. But some debtors fled, Pham told FBI informants, so the ring tightened up by demanding cars, jewelry and other possessions to back up the loans.

Even the ones who ran away, Pham told an FBI informant in 1992, probably would not escape the gang's reach. He told of a woman who had fled to Hong Kong, owing him a $30,000 gambling debt.

"Our people are over there," he said. "They know that she is in Kowloon...They control the operation in Kowloon and the operation in Los Angeles...I just didn't give a loan to her without a means of getting it back...I don't worry about that $30,000."

Although the files described a variety of crimes allegedly committed by Pham and others, the government decided to prosecute them for drug offenses in order to get the stiffest sentences. Most, including Pham, have pleaded guilty, and one of those in the ring got a 10-year prison sentence.

Pham is to be sentenced next month. One of his attorneys, Nina Wilder, rejected allegations of Pham's gang ties last week and said it was noteworthy that the government charged him only with a drug offense.

"Those are simply police reports," she said of the FBI documents. "They can put anything they want in there."

To investigators, the Pham case showed the ease with which organized crime penetrated a card club. But loan-sharking and drug-dealing are just two prongs of the problem, law officers say.

Authorities have linked murders, money laundering and robberies at Silicon Valley companies to casino gambling. And crime has touched the front office: Executives of two leading clubs, including Garden City, were imprisoned in recent years in skimming and political payoff scandals.

In the robberies, authorities say, gangs seek out workers at high-technology businesses who frequent casinos, get acquainted with them and loan them money to gamble. In return, the workers give the gangs inside information on their factories and on how to steal valuable computer components, usually semiconductor chips.

"Many of the connections between gangs and entrepreneurs or employees of these high-tech companies are made in these cardrooms," said U.S. Attorney Michael Yamaguchi. "What they typically look for is someone who has a lot of money to gamble, and it may be a spouse who is flashing a lot of jewelry."

Authorities are divided on the casinos' dedication to checking crime. Some privately say that the quest for profits leads managers to wink at loansharking and other offenses, while others praise clubs for bolstering surveillance and taking other crime-fighting steps.

San Jose police Lieutenant Phil Beltran has both kind and critical words for that city's two big clubs, Garden City and the Bay 101 Club.

"I see a concentrated effort on the part of the clubs to tighten themselves up," he says. But he adds: "Sometimes, the clubs don't know what's going on under their noses. They say it's not so, but we know it."

Casinos see much of the criticism as distorted or inaccurate and blame anti-gambling forces for bad publicity. Police in some cities with cardrooms side with the casinos, offering statistics in an effort to demonstrate that serious crime is minimal.

"In our city, cardrooms don't cause us any more police problems than any other business would draw," says San Bruno Police Chief Joe Palla.

That community has two cardrooms, including 80-year-old Artichoke Joe's which recently won city permission to increase to a size that would make it among the largest in Northern California.

San Pablo Police Chief Douglas Krathwohl is a stout defender of Casino San Pablo, a flashy new club that would look right at home on the Las Vegas Strip. In the casino's first year, he says, police have responded to about 60 calls, about 50 of them for minor offenses like rowdyism, petty theft and vandalism.

Krathwohl says that in view of what the casino pays in annual taxes—about $4 million—he is willing to put up with that kind of a problem. San Pablo needs the money, he says, so it "boils down to financial survival."

But law officers who have had troubles with big casinos don't share Krathwohl's views. They say that crimes like extortion and robbery often go unreported because victims fear retribution.

"The only time these crimes get reported is when there is violence involved," says an officer who has watched card clubs for years. "Over half of these crimes go unreported."

In San Jose's experience, a 1995 Police Department report said, clubs also try to hide crime. An investigation found that when offenses occurred around Garden City Casino several years ago, club security people handled them alone. Garden City spokeswoman Nanci Williams downplayed the reporting failures as out of date. The club is under new management, she said, and working closely with San Jose police to keep itself as clean as possible.

Garden City General Manager Paul Fontaine said he was unaware of the Pham case but added that the club has gone to substantial lengths to try to keep out unsavory people. One move, he said, was to hire a former member of the San

Francisco Police Department's gang task force to watch for known ring members.

"We monitor them, and if they should do anything detrimental to the club, we exclude them," he says. "We keep a detailed file on them."

Fontaine said Garden City officials meet often with San Jose police to share intelligence and concerns.

"We know what's going on," he says. "We just can't have detrimental acts. We just don't let it happen."

Attorney General Dan Lungren argues that California will never get a strong hand on crime spawned by cardrooms until the Legislature votes money to beef up oversight. Supporters of tighter state control on casinos are backing legislation that would give Lungren greater regulatory power. Some provisions would let the state review casinos' security, while at the same time granting cardrooms wider authority to evict unsavory patrons.

While endorsing the steps, some local authorities seek more. Proposals include requiring casinos to keep better track of cash exchanges in order to combat money-laundering and lowering amounts that can be bet to discourage loansharking. Even symbolic steps like paying security officers more and encouraging top executives to spend time on the casino floor might help check crime, says Sergeant Spitze.

Since a narcotics raid at San Jose's Bay 101 club last February, there have been no major incidents at Northern California's casinos. To Beltran, that's gratifying—but no cause for cheer.

"It is," he says, "an uneasy calm."

Gambling With the Mob?

Wise Guys
Have Set Their Sights on
the Booming Indian Casino Business

James Popkin
U.S. News & World Report, **August 23, 1993**

Seated in the largest Senate hearing room with a hood over his head to protect his identity, the witness identified only as "Marty" had some confessions to make. Not only had he helped the mob set up and run a high-stakes bingo hall on an Indian reservation, he testified, but he had padded expenses and robbed the tribe of over $600,000 a year.

But even Marty's sensational tales of filling bingo balls with helium and awarding $60,000 cars to paid shills paled in comparison to his next news flash. Marty told members of the Senate Select Committee on Indian Affairs that 12 other Indian bingo halls also were controlled by the mob. "Organized crime is destroying the Indian reservation," he said in a slow, mechanical baritone, his voice deliberately altered through the use of a special machine.

Four years later, the leaders of the Indian gambling industry are still smarting. Marty's apocalyptic visions of Mafia domination have been proven wrong, they argue, adding that Indian-owned casinos and bingo halls are more heavily regulated than the glitz palaces in Atlantic City and Las Vegas. But while it's true that the industry has grown much more sophisticated and has weeded out the most venal operators, many questionable characters remain. From dozens of interviews with federal, state and local law-enforcement officials and from documents obtained through the Freedom of Information Act, *U.S. News* has learned of a number of cases that raise serious doubts about the integrity and inviolability of Indian casinos.

The New Buffalo

Devastated by unemployment, substandard housing and schools and crippling alcoholism, many Indians have come to see gambling as "the new buffalo"—the first true economic opportunity in two centuries. But buffalo never paid dividends like a one-armed bandit. In Connecticut, the sprawling Foxwoods Casino owned by the Mashantucket Pequots could conceivably gross $1 billion this year and net half that amount. On the Shakopee Mdewakanton Dakota reservation near Minneapolis, the Mystic Lake casino takes in so much cash that tribal members sometimes receive dividend checks for up to $20,000 a person per month, one official with the Bureau of Indian Affairs says. And just last month near Syracuse, N.Y., the Oneida Indians opened the $10 million Turning Stone Casino, expected to rake in well over $100 million a year.

Now that 73 tribes in 19 states offer or will soon offer full-scale casino gambling, the big boys have taken notice. Atlantic City casino owner Donald Trump recently sued the U.S. government for allegedly giving an unfair advantage to tribes setting up casinos. And he's out to prove the fledgling industry is corrupt. "A lot of the reservations are being, at least to a certain extent, run by organized crime," says Trump. "There's no protection. It's become a joke."

Mobsters did, in fact, prey upon Indian gambling during the 1980s. Besides Marty, whose real name was Stewart Siegel and who managed a California bingo hall for the Barona Indians before he died of cancer, Indian gambling's cast of characters was like something out of an Edward G. Robinson movie. Just this spring, for example, reputed Chicago mob boss John "No Nose" DiFronzo and his gambling expert, Donald "The Wizard of Odds" Angelini, were convicted of conspiracy and fraud in a failed attempt to take over gambling operations at the Rincon Reservation near San Diego in the late '80s. The Chicagoans had hoped to skim profits and launder mob money, FBI wiretaps show. In 1980, California's Cabazon Indian tribe hired as their poker-room manager one Rocco Zangari, identified as a mobster in Senate testimony. He was subsequently fired. Later, after tribal Vice Chairman Alfred Alvarez complained to local newspapers about poker-room skimming, Alvarez and two others were shot dead; the case has never been solved.

"There's probably been a learning curve, and people have been burned," says Rick Hill of the National Indian Gaming Association. But Las Vegas was an open town for mobsters in the 1930s, he adds, policed only by a sheriff. "You always have to look at things from a historical perspective."

Trump's hyperbole notwithstanding, the vast majority of the 175 total Indian casinos and bingo halls are honest and clean. Many employ Las Vegas or Atlantic City pros and have vigilant in-house security teams. Several management companies are publicly traded and have passed overlapping layers of government scrutiny. The FBI does not see a "coordinated, concerted effort" by organized-crime families to raid the Indian gambling industry, says Jim Moody, chief of the FBI's organized-crime section. There are no "publicly known" cases of current mob infiltration.

But the threat remains. The bureau has six ongoing investigations—one more than when Moody testified on Capitol Hill just a few months ago. And when asked which crime families are interested in Indian gambling, Moody replied: "I don't know any that aren't."

The Pittsburgh Road Paver

The FBI is investigating a Pennsylvania asphalt-company owner who manages a major casino in Minnesota and is expanding into tribal gambling in California, Oklahoma and Ontario, Canada, U.S. News has learned. Angelo Medure, 64, president of Gaming World International, has no criminal record and has passed the background checks required to manage the Shooting Star Casino in Mahnomen, Minn., owned by the White Earth Band of Chippewa. No charges have been filed against him. But the FBI became suspicious when it learned Medure leases a New Castle, Pa., warehouse to a pasta firm that was run in the 1980s by reputed mobsters.

The Pennsylvania Crime Commission says that Henry "Zebo" Zottola, 57, was president of Rocca's Italian Foods and that Louis Raucci Sr., 63, was an investor and employee. Zottola helps collect payments for the Michael Genovese crime family from local loan sharks, bookies and drug dealers, the commission says. Raucci was convicted in 1990 on racketeering, narcotics and tax violations and is serving a 27-year jail sentence.

In an interview, Medure initially denied knowing Raucci or Zottola. Later, he said he had met Zottola at the pasta plant several times but claims he was unaware of Zottola's background. Confidential telephone records obtained by *U.S. News* confirm their relationship. A 24-page summary of calls made in 1986 from Zottola's Pittsburgh home reveals that Zottola called Medure's house and his trailer home in New Castle six times on March 12, 1986. On May 9, Zottola called Medure's condominium in Pompano Beach, Fla., and Medure's construction company. Medure says he has no organized-crime links and claims Zottola simply called to discuss warehouse remodeling plans.

Zottola acknowledged last week that he called Medure repeatedly in 1986 to discuss the warehouse. He admits being friends with men who the crime commission says are Pittsburgh mobsters but claims he has no link to the Mafia and is just an honest carpet salesman.

Although Zottola never admitted it to local FBI agents when they questioned him three months ago about Medure, the calls did not stop in 1986. Zottola called Medure about eight months ago to discuss selling him video-poker machines to be used at the Minnesota casino. Medure confirmed the call but says he told Zottola he was not interested. "[Medure] told me that anything he put on that reservation had to be approved by the state of Minnesota. And I just forgot about it after that," Zottola adds.

The White Earth tribe has had some curious business dealings in the past. In 1987, before Medure became involved, Carmen Ricci sold 30 video-poker machines to the tribe. New

Jersey officials describe Ricci as an associate of the Nicodemo Scarfo crime family. "At that time they were legitimate businessmen," tribal Chairman Darrell "Chip" Wadena says.

Medure profits handsomely from his casino deal. His firm gets 35 percent of casino profits—at least $3 million a year. Chairman Wadena fought to increase Medure's take by 5 percent, at his own tribe's expense, but a federal mediator refused. Medure has plans to manage casinos for the Hopland Band of Pomo Indians and the Cloverdale Pomo Indians in Northern California, and the Ratportage First Nation near Kenora in Ontario. His firm also plans to manage a bingo hall, set to open this week, for the Seneca-Cayuga tribe in Miami, Okla.

The Strip-Bar Owner

Restaurant owner Robert Sabes was well known in Minneapolis as a millionaire businessman. So locals were hardly surprised when he created a successful casino management firm called Gaming Corp. of America. But troubles began this spring when Mississippi gaming regulators learned that Sabes owns a topless bar in Minneapolis where the entertainment was managed by Michael Peter, a flashy South Florida millionaire with a nationwide chain of striptease bars called Solid Gold. Peter was indicted in 1991 on extortion and kidnaping charges, and the case is pending in state court. Federal agents seized thousands of Peter's documents at about the same time, citing concern over possible organized-crime ties. No federal charges have been filed.

Sabes denies any mob links and says he had "an arm's length" relationship with Peter. But the embarrassment and the licensing delays to come persuaded Sabes to sell his Gaming Corp. stock last April and leave the publicly traded firm. Although one tribe quickly cut all ties to the restaurateur, others continue to seek his business. Early last month, Sabes won preliminary approval from Arizona's Yavapai-Apaches to manage their proposed casino north of Phoenix.

New evidence of a more troubling relationship may jeopardize those plans, too. In testimony to the Wisconsin Winnebago gaming commission released this month, Sabes admits also doing business with James Williams, a partner in Peter's strip-bar empire and once a major bingo hall operator for Indian tribes and charities from California to Florida. Williams was convicted in 1987 of failing to pay taxes on some $300,000 he earned from bingo halls. Florida police records call him a "close associate" of Anthony Accetturo's, whom the FBI has identified as a capo, or boss, of the Thomas Luchese crime family of New York. Williams, who did not return phone calls, admits in the police files only to meeting Accetturo three times in the 1970s.

In a recent interview, Sabes admitted that he signed papers with Williams as early as Nov. 9, 1988. That was just four months before Williams was locked up, prison officials say. But he says he did not learn of Williams's conviction or alleged Mafia ties until 1990.

The Bingo Paper Supplier

When Florida's Miccosukee Indians opened a 2,000-seat bingo hall west of Miami in 1991, they hired Tamiami Partners to run it. Two years later the tribe kicked the firm out, alleging mob ties. Tamiami partner Cye Mandel denies the charges and has sued the tribe for cutting him out of the venture, which last year grossed $35 million. One thing is sure: Tamiami did sign a contract with a bingo paper supplier authorities have linked to the mob.

After a bidding process, Tamiami began buying supplies from Frank Nannicola of Warren, Ohio. Nannicola is the son-in-law of Charles Imburgia, who, according to the Pennsylvania Crime Commission, is a member of the Genovese crime family in Pittsburgh. A 1992 crime commission report claims certain bingo operations in the Youngstown, Ohio, area "are obligated to purchase bingo supplies from Nannicola."

Nannicola says his firm sells supplies in 25 states and got the Tamiami contract because of superior service and price. He denies that his father-in-law or his business has mob ties: "The Pennsylvania Crime Commission should get some new employees and some new information."

Despite the allegations, the National Indian Gaming Commission has never done a background check on Nannicola Wholesale or Tamiami Partners. One reason: Although Congress created the commission five years ago to regulate Indian gaming, its rules didn't take effect until six months ago. The commission has a massive backlog of old and new management contracts to review.

Just such snags prompted members of Congress to meet this summer to discuss tightening Indian gambling laws, and a new Senate bill likely will be introduced next month. National Indian Gaming Association Chairman Rick Hill says the tribes want the cleanest industry possible. But they also want to ensure that a few questionable characters do not bring ruin to an industry that employs thousands and has helped tribes build much-needed schools, hospitals and homes. "It's a bread-and-butter issue," Hill says. "We need Indian gaming to survive."

Twin Cities Man Pleads Guilty in Las Vegas

Chris Ison

Star Tribune, August 30, 1995

When Twin Cities businessman Deil Gustafson joined mob bosses from three cities in federal prison 12 years ago, it was supposed to mark the end of one of the most intense organized-crime probes in the country.

As the alleged front man in a mob scheme to take over a group of Las Vegas casinos, the former banker and DFL activist had become entangled in a web of hidden ownerships, off-the-books transactions and check kiting, most designed to hide the true owners of Gustafson's Tropicana Casino and Hotel.

Now, more than 20 years after he bought the towering casino on the Vegas strip, the Trop's shady past has landed him in the hands of federal authorities again.

Gustafson has pleaded guilty to bankruptcy fraud, according to documents unsealed Tuesday in Las Vegas. His undisclosed plea two weeks ago, and Tuesday's indictment of five others, culminates a four-year federal investigation that includes allegations of money laundering, fraud, hidden ownerships and even death threats.

Gustafson, the former real estate magnate and deputy director of Hubert Humphrey's 1960 presidential campaign, is expected to testify against the five alleged coconspirators in return for a lighter prison sentence. One of them is Twin Cities attorney John Jagiela, according to an indictment also unsealed in Las Vegas Tuesday. He handled legal matters for the company that operated Gustafson's Tropicana.

He is charged with falsifying documents and conspiring to cover up payments to alleged Mafia associates who had hidden interests in the casino.

The case has tentacles reaching back to Gustafson's sale of the Tropicana to Ramada Inc. in 1979, just as federal agents were closing in on their original investigation into mob skimming of profits and secret ownership of the casino.

The sale was tied up for several years in litigation over how much Gustafson and his co-owners were owed from the transaction. Gustafson, meanwhile, went to prison in 1983 as agents wrapped up their organized-crime probe.

He completed his 40-month sentence in 1987 and quickly landed on his feet, winning the court case three years later. He and his partners were to be given $34 million for the casino sale, but they couldn't get all that money. Their company that ran the Tropicana, Hotel Conquistador Inc. (HCI), had gone bankrupt and owed millions to creditors.

They apparently also owed money to hidden mob associates, according to search warrants filed in the recent investigation. And alleged secret payments to those associates are what sparked the new probe leading to Tuesday's indictments.

As federal agents began to learn how the $34 million was being distributed, some familiar names started to surface, names that first emerged during the investigation that landed Gustafson and organized crime bosses in prison a decade earlier.

One search warrant affidavit filed in the recent case described an intricate system of payments to phony creditors and the laundering of more than $1 million, part of which was allegedly used to pay off one of the Trop's mob-connected "silent partners."

Tuesday's indictment names Nicholas Tanno, who allegedly represented organized crime interests in Kansas City and Cleveland. The indictment says that he demanded more than $1 million in payments from Gustafson and indicated that "Gustafson and his daughter would be killed if [Gustafson] refused to pay the money." Gustafson paid, and Jagiela, the Twin Cities attorney, helped conceal the payment, falsifying records and lying to an FBI agent, according to the indictment.

Also charged in the indictment were brothers Edward and Fred Doumani, Las Vegas hotel owners who also held an interest in HCI, the company that owned the Tropicana. Harold Gewerter, a Nevada attorney who represented HCI, also was indicted. And so was Jack Urich, a California oil magnate who tried to buy into the Tropicana but was rejected by Nevada officials because of his associations with a Mafia associate.

Like Tanno's, Urich's name surfaced in the original Tropicana case, but he steadfastly denied wrongdoing and was never charged.

FBI special agent Joseph Degnan said in a search warrant affidavit filed in the recent probe that he "believes that the principals of HCI utilized [a middle man] to funnel money to Jack Urich and possibly other people who were owed money by HCI or had hidden interests in HCI and whose identities were intentionally concealed by HCI from the bankruptcy court."

None of the five men indicted have been arrested, Johnson, the prosecutor, said Tuesday. All are expected to appear at an initial federal court hearing in Las Vegas, which has not been scheduled.

Jagiela couldn't be reached for comment late Tuesday. A secretary at Gustafson's office at the Flour Exchange Building in downtown Minneapolis said he was out of town and unavailable.

Gustafson, who pleaded guilty Aug. 16, has not been sentenced, but could face substantial prison time. Federal guidelines call for a sentence of 27 to 33 months. But prosecutors have agreed to request less time if Gustafson cooperates fully by supplying information and testifying in court.

Gustafson also has agreed to pay back taxes to the IRS totaling $700,000, according to the plea agreement, which was unsealed Tuesday.

Jagiela, who has worked at several major law firms in the Twin Cities, was suspended from law practice for six months last year after information about his involvement in the Tropicana case surfaced. He was reinstated this past June.

Part V

Taking the Saps

Advertising
and Other Tricks of the Trade

The odds of winning a jackpot are much worse than the odds of being struck by lightning, but you'd never know it from the inescapable barrage of billboards, radio ads and television spots blanketing the countryside. Those who run the various types of gambling institutions uniformly claim that gambling is strictly voluntary, that people spend their money because they like to gamble. If that were true, those entities wouldn't be spending hundreds of millions of dollars every year to push paper tickets and spins of the roulette wheel.

The tactics are often outrageous. Lottery directors across the country regularly target the poor, minorities and compulsive gamblers when they advertise, conveniently leaving out any mention of the realistic odds of winning (states are, incredibly enough, exempt from truth-in-advertising laws). In one particularly galling example, the Illinois State Lottery placed a billboard in one of Chicago's poorest neighborhoods that read "Your Ticket Out of Here."

Casinos have their own tricks, as James Popkin points out in the following *U.S. News & World Report* article "Tricks of the Trade." Once the catchy jingles and colorful billboards bring consumers through the door, they are subject to a whole host of manipulative tactics. Numerous casinos pump specially designed smells into gambling areas so people will stay longer and spend more. Others use scientifically chosen colors and payout patterns to draw and keep patrons' attention. They go to all this trouble to distract gamblers from the obvious: Gambling is a losing proposition.

Everyone's a Loser

How Lottery Ads
Entice the Wrong People to Gamble

Joshua Wolf Shenk
July/August, 1995

Tom had been playing the lottery for two years when God started whispering in his ear. At first, Tom (who asked that his last name be withheld) would spend just a few dollars a week. He had his regular numbers, and he'd play them when he thought of it.

But then, he says, on the days that he hadn't planned on playing, the word would come from Heaven: Your number is coming *tonight*. Fear would strike him like ice water on the neck: "I'd think, 'I'm not going to win it. I don't have the [money] on that number.'" So he'd rush out to play his regular number, and many more. Before long, he was spending $300 a week on tickets.

"It was 'A Dollar and a Dream'; 'Hey, You Never know,'" he says, repeating the advertising slogans of the New York lottery. Tom pauses. "Those were good come-ons."

It's no accident that the voices inside Tom's head echoed lottery ads. They're extremely effective. And they're everywhere: on the radio and TV, in bus shelters and on billboards, even in mailings sent straight to homes. The message is simple: Play the lottery and get rich. Get rich, and all your problems will be solved. The New York lottery takes in more than $2 billion in sales each year, and it spends $30 million each year on advertising to keep the cash rolling in.

State lotteries target anyone who might cough up a dollar (or $10 or $20) for the chance to strike it rich. Conveniently silent on the odds, these ads send the message that hard work and patience is for suckers. In the process, the ads help wring billions of dollars from the most vulnerable "customers" possible—the poor and the addicted.

Criticism of state lotteries runs a wide gamut. Some say the state shouldn't even *allow* gambling, much less conduct it. Others argue that gambling should be left in private hands. Still others believe that the state should run lotteries for roughly the same reasons many states run liquor stores: to keep the business controlled and clean, and to make money for the state.

Regardless of where you stand on these important questions, though, one thing should be clear: The advertising that entices Americans to spend tens of billions of dollars on lottery tickets each year is deceitful and corrosive. It is the only form of advertising unburdened by state and federal truth-in-advertising standards. The fact that it comes from the state—which ought to encourage people's strengths, not prey on their weaknesses—makes it all the more foul.

Today, 37 states and the District of Columbia have instituted lotteries, and that number is likely to grow. "Quite simply, states need the revenue," explains David Gale, executive director of the North American Association of State and Provincial Lotteries. "Every dollar raised by the lottery is a dollar you don't need to get from taxes." Across the country, $34 billion in lottery tickets were sold in 1994. In Texas, the lottery contributed $935 million to the state's budget. In New York, the figure was $1.01 billion. As states have become dependent on lottery revenue, the pressure to keep people playing has become relentless. "Marketing is absolutely essential," Gale says. "Lottery tickets are no different than any other product. Your market will lose interest after a while. You have to keep after them."

Like any sophisticated business, lotteries target the specific groups of people most susceptible to suggestion. The Iowa lottery's media plan, for example, contains the following statement of objective: "To target our message demographically against those that we know to be heavy users."

One such target is the poor. The charge that lotteries are regressive—that is, hitting lower-income residents the hardest—makes intuitive sense, since the pitch of wealthy fantasies clearly resonates most strongly among those who are least affluent. "There's absolutely no question about it," says Charles Clotfelter, a Duke University economist and a leading authority on lotteries. According to a study by the Heartland Institute, a conservative think tank, the poor spend more money than the non-poor on lotteries—not only as a percentage of their income, but also in absolute terms. Blacks and Hispanics also tend to p¹ay more often than whites.

I worked two summers at an Ohio convenience store that sold lottery tickets, and my experience there confirms these findings. The store drew customers from all socioeconomic backgrounds, but lottery players fell into distinct categories. On a normal day, the lottery patrons were mostly working-class blacks. When the jackpots for Super Lotto got sky-high, some wealthier folks joined the lines. But the staple customers— those who spent five, 20, or 40 dollars a day on daily numbers and scratch-off games—were the same people every day: not executives or store managers playing for kicks, but postal workers and retirees on Social Security. You'll see the same trend at almost any lottery outlet. You'll also notice that the same stores almost invariably sell liquor and cigarettes. Choose your poison.

The image of miserable working people magically transported to lives of wealth and ease is a staple of lottery ads. A billboard once placed in a slum of Chicago read simply: "YOUR TICKET OUT OF HERE." An ad for the D.C. lottery shows a man "before" the lottery—with matted hair, stubble on his face, and glasses—and "after"—freshly washed and clean-shaven, wearing a tuxedo, and holding the program for a theater performance. The copy reads: "Just One Ticket...And It Could Happen to You." An ad for the Michigan lottery shows a college kid piloting a Lear jet. Then it cuts to him day-dreaming on the job at a fast food restaurant. "Thirty new Lotto millionaires were created last year," the announcer states. "Play the Lotto, and you could win the stuff dreams are made of."

Lottery ads also go after gambling addicts, using a message tuned to their weaknesses. About 5 percent of the population is susceptible to compulsive gambling, according to Dr. Valerie

Lorenz, executive director of the Compulsive Gambling Center in Baltimore. In many cases, she says, lottery ads help tip these people over the edge.

Remember Tom's greatest fear, that his number would fall on a day he hadn't bet? This is one of the defining characteristics of compulsive gamblers, and it's a button that lotteries push incessantly. "Don't forget to play every day," the Pennsylvania lottery ad says. Many ads picture disheartened would-be winners whose numbers came up on a day they declined or forgot to play. One ad for Tri-State Megabucks (in New Hampshire, Maine, and Vermont), for example, shows a pathetic man grilling hamburgers on a fire escape, while scenes of wealth and grandeur flash by. The theme is set to the tune of "It Had to Be You."

> It could have been you.
> It could have been you.
> Countin' the dough,
> Ready to go, on that three-month cruise.
> Walkin' in style, down easy street,
> Wearin' a smile, it could have been sweet.
> But what can I say?
> You just didn't play.
> It could have been youuuuu!

The theme of magical, instant transformation also lures problem gamblers. "They live in a very painful world," says Dr. Lorenz. "They want to escape into fantasy, and they want it instantly." And, of course, the sheer regularity of the ads is a curse to addicts trying to stay on the straight-and-narrow. "I hear this all the time from lottery addicts who are in recovery," Lorenz says. "They'll cover their ears or their heads. They'll say, 'I wish I could leave the state.' But that wouldn't help. It's all over the country."

The ads never mention the losers. Tom Cummings, executive director of the Massachusetts Council on Compulsive Gambling, told me about two women he has been counseling. "One lost her house after going $40,000 in debt playing the lottery," he said. "The other gambled away money that was supposed to pay for her daughter's education. All on the lottery."

Lotteries aren't alone in suggesting that their product has magical qualities—that's the art of advertising. But lottery ads take a prize when it comes to their systematic distortion. Because the lotteries are chartered by state legislatures, they're untouchable by federal regulators and they consider state regulators their colleagues in public service. This allows lotteries to conceal the astronomical odds against winning and inflate the size of jackpots.

Consider a 1993 California radio spot profiling a lottery winner: "John Padgett went to bed on Saturday night a regular guy," the announcer says. "When he woke up, he was worth $11 million. That's because he's Super Lotto winner number 610."

Well, not quite. Padgett did win an $11.5 million jackpot. But that's not *worth* $11.5 million. Any prize over a million dollars is paid out over 20 years. Padgett's annual payment came to $575,000. After taxes, the actual yearly award is worth around $400,000. And the lost value—due to both inflation ($400,000 will be worth far less in 2013 than it is today) and lost interest—is significant.

It may be hard to sympathize with someone receiving a $400,000 check every year. But this ad—and nearly every state uses a similar pitch—is clearly misleading. The government would never allow similar distortions from private sector advertisers.

Finance companies, for example, are explicitly forbidden to air commercials that feature investors who have earned vast sums of money with the message, "It could be you." But lotteries do just that. "I was probably going to have to go back to work to make ends meet," Kentucky lottery winner Denise Golden says in one ad. "And now I won't have to...It's a dream come true."

Lotteries are also exempt from Federal Trade Commission truth-in-advertising standards and rules that, to give just one example, require contests and sweepstakes to clearly state the odds against winning in every advertisement. Omitting the odds is a crucial element of lotteries' media strategy, since they're trying to convince people that if they play long enough, they are certain to hit the jackpot. "Sooner than later," says an ad for the West Virginia lottery, "You're gonna win!" "We won't stop until everyone's a millionaire," the New York lottery promises.

A clue as to how far lotteries exceed the bounds that constrain other advertisers is indicated by a report from the National Association of Broadcasters issued in 1975. Three tactics seemed clearly out of bounds, the NAB concluded:

1. [Indicating] what fictitious winners may do, hope to do or have done with their winnings.

2. [Using] unqualified or inaccurate language regarding potential winners' winnings (e.g. "There's a pot of gold for those who buy lottery tickets"; "Buy a ticket and be a winner.")

3. [Utilizing] approaches which praise people who buy lottery tickets or denigrate people who do not buy tickets.

Today's lotteries hold themselves to no such standards. The only rule is to produce maximum profit. Even in Virginia and Texas, two states that forbid their lotteries to "induce people to play," ads make gambling seem fun and glamorous. Missouri originally required all its lottery ads to include a disclaimer: "This message…is not intended to induce any person to participate in the lottery or purchase a lottery ticket." The disclaimer was dropped in 1988. It was thought to be hurting sales.

Lotteries defend themselves against criticism by citing the revenue they raise. They also advertise to publicize their role in funding state projects. (Not only does this approach bolster political support, it's also a shrewd ploy to hook more players. Gambling is fun—and it's also a public service!)

Each state has its own slogan: "When Colorado plays, everybody wins." "The Missouri lottery: It makes life a little richer for all of us." The premise of these ads—and a crucial element of lotteries' popularity—is that money goes to improving favorite areas of state spending, like schools or parks. But this is a mere accounting trick. Ohio claims that its lottery revenue goes toward education, for example. "But that doesn't mean that the budget for education grows by that much," David Gale explains. "What happens is, the legislature budgets this much for education. They see the lottery will contribute this much.

So they take the money they would have spent on education and put it to other uses."

Most states avoid the fiction altogether and say outright that the money goes to the general fund. But that doesn't stop lotteries from claiming credit for the very best of state government. On its 20th anniversary, the Maryland lottery ran a series of "public service" ads. One pictured a nurse holding an infant, saying the baby would get better care because of the Maryland lottery. Another ad in the series gave credit to the lottery for the high school graduation of an inner-city black teenager.

It is true that lottery profits go to state treasuries. But so do taxes. Taxes are also honestly raised and reflect community decisions about how to fairly distribute burdens and responsibilities. In the current political climate, raising lottery revenue is a political virtue; raising taxes is political death. Naturally, politicians choose the easy route. New York Governor George Pataki recently announced plans for an enormous tax cut. He intends to make up the loss in revenue through the introduction of "five minute keno" in liquor stores and bars, which is expected to net the state $115 million per year.

Lotteries defend themselves by pointing out the obvious: No one is forced to buy a lottery ticket. "I get so angry when people say they should decide how [others] should spend their money," says Teresa La Fleur, who publishes books and a magazine for the lottery industry. "Unless we decide it's wrong to gamble, it's just a fact of life that people are going to make choices with their money."

But states don't merely allow, or provide, gambling. They stimulate it. In addition to running ads, some states even conduct direct-mail campaigns, sending coupons for free tickets via mail. In a typical campaign, cited in *Selling Hope: State Lotteries in America*, by Clotfelter and co-author Phillip Cook, 35 to 40 percent of the coupons were redeemed for lottery tickets. One-third of those who redeemed the coupons were new players; one-third of those new players began to play regularly.

Considering the addictiveness of lotteries, these types of promotions are inexcusable. Of the nearly 40,000 calls to the

Council on Compulsive Gambling in New Jersey last year, for example, 52 percent complained of addiction to lottery games. Imagine the outcry if Phillip Morris sent free packs of cigarettes through the mail.

In fact, the parallel between cigarettes and lottery tickets is uncanny. That's why both have been the subject of strict limits on advertising. Until 1974, when Congress repealed a ban on the promotion of gambling in the mass media, TV stations couldn't so much as mention winning numbers. Now, of course, TV is the most popular medium of advertising. Besides the many commercials, lottery drawings are on television, and a number of states have half-hour game shows centered around the lottery.

Congressman Jim McCrery, a Republican from Louisiana, has introduced legislation requiring the Federal Trade Commission to impose truth-in-advertising standards on lotteries. That would be a start. But a more dramatic step—banning ads altogether—is in order.

Lottery ads don't just sell a product. They sell a way of life. One ad for the Washington state lottery shows a line of workers punching their time clock. "The true joys in life," the announcer says, "are not found in the empty pursuit of pleasure, but in the accomplishments realized through one's own hard labor. For nothing satisfies the soul so much as honest toil, and seeing through a job well done." Then the man at the end of the line takes his time sheet and throws it out the window. "Of course having a whole bunch of money's not bad either."

When will the public officials stop for a moment and listen to what they're saying—that hard work and patience are for suckers, that civic virtue is a function of how much you spend on the lottery? "Even in these cynical times," says Clotfelter, "government has some moral capital. So when the government says, 'Children, stay in school'; 'Husbands, don't beat your wives'—these have some value to them. If you take that capital and use it [the way lotteries do], one has to ask, does this serve the intention of the state?"

The Big Lottery Gamble

Iris Cohen Selinger

Reprinted with permission from the
May 10, 1993 issue of *Advertising Age*
Copyright © Crain Communications Inc. 1993

"Hey, you never know."

That's the memorable ad slogan for New York Lotto. Gamblers sometimes recall it while talking to Dr. Eileen A. Epstein, among other memories harder for them to talk about—the debt they've incurred, the families and friends they've lost—all because of their addiction to games of chance, some of them government-sponsored and made more appealing by advertising.

"Advertising feeds into the fantasy," says Dr. Epstein, a gambling counselor at the John F. Kennedy Medical Center in Edison, N.J.

Seducing players into believing the fantasy is the goal of lottery advertising. It seems to be working quite nicely, judging by the rush of states into the lottery business.

But what about what the advertising doesn't tell players? For instance, that a player has a much greater chance of being struck by lightning than he does winning big in the lottery—1 in 1.9 million odds for lightning vs. 1 in 12 million for the top prize in most lotteries. Or that the percentage of money going to winners is smaller in lotteries than in just about any other form of gambling? Or that playing the lottery can be hazardous to your mental health, as well as your pocketbook?

These are questions being raised increasingly these days by a budding grassroots movement against lotteries and the way they're advertised.

"Lottery advertising is an absolute sham," says Donald Conkey, founder of the Georgia Alliance Against Gambling, one of several groups that oppose Georgia's lottery, scheduled to start this summer.

As lottery advertising continues to increase and draw more public scrutiny, critics say we could see a replay of the 1970s and 1980s debate over cigarette and alcohol advertising and the subsequent restrictions and warning labels.

"I think it's just a matter of time before we challenge the advertising," says Wisconsin state Sen. Fred Risser, who doesn't like the lottery ads he sees in his state.

"We should be as restricting with lottery advertising as we are with liquor advertising," he says.

Minnesota state Sen. John Marty earlier this year tried unsuccessfully to ban lottery advertising entirely in the state. "I know it would reduce what the lottery makes, but I don't know that the state should be in this business," Sen. Marty said in introducing his legislation.

Illegal in all states until 1964, lotteries have become big business as financially strapped states seek revenue sources more palatable than outright taxes. Last year, they racked up sales of $21.9 billion in the 34 states, plus the District of Columbia, where they were offered. Mississippi and Nebraska, as well as Georgia, will start lotteries this year, helping to boost lotto sales to a projected $24.2 billion, up another 11% from last year. An Oklahoma group, with the blessing of Gov. David Walters, last month launched a petition drive to create a lottery there. By the end of the decade, every state but Utah and Nevada will have lotteries, observers say.

In addition, existing lotteries are expanding their offerings to video lotteries, keno and other spinoff games in an effort to keep revenue rising.

Spending on lottery advertising has increased steadily, to $286 million last year, making lottos one of the more attractive growth accounts for ad agencies. As a group, lotteries rank among the top 50 advertisers in the country, spending more than such heavy hitters as Nissan Motor Corp. USA, Colgate-Palmolive Co., American Express Co. and Nike. California, Florida, New York, Illinois and Virginia each spend $20 million to $30 million a year on lottery advertising, sizable accounts that look especially good to ad agencies in today's weak advertising economy.

In the past, lottery business was awarded mostly to small local agencies, largely because states wanted to keep the accounts within the state. But lately, large agencies have jumped onto the lotto bandwagon.

J. Walter Thompson USA, San Francisco, last year snagged the California State Lottery from Los Angeles-based Daily & Associates, for example, while McCann-Erickson Worldwide, Seattle, won the Washington State Lottery from regional shop Borders, Perrin & Norrander.

"The lottery account is like a consumer entertainment product—it's very visible, it's fun and it allows for top drawer creative," says Sharon Sharp, California State Lottery marketing director, who had some 100 agencies vying for the $29.5 million business last year.

But critics dispute the idea that lotteries are mere entertainment and that the advertising used to sell lottery tickets is benign.

"Lotteries by any definition are a form of gambling," says Henry Lesier, an expert on compulsive gambling and chairman of the criminal justice department of Illinois State University.

"It is the most habituating of all gambling," says Vicki Abt, a professor of sociology at Penn State and author of *The Business of Risk: Commercial Gambling in Mainstream America.* "More repeaters do it consistently than any other form of gambling," she adds.

What's more, lottery critics claim the games amount to a severely regressive "tax." In one of several studies with similar findings, the Heartland Institute, a conservative Chicago think tank, concluded that "state lotteries place a greater relative burden on low-income families because low-income groups spend a higher percentage of their income on lottery tickets than do high-income groups."

"This disproportionate play," the institute said, "is almost certainly exacerbated by misleading and targeted advertising."

To buttress their complaints, critics often cite what must be the nadir of lottery advertising, a 1986 outdoor board on

Chicago's depressed West Side that proclaimed the Illinois Lottery to be "Your way out."

It's such ads, claims Georgia critic Mr. Conkey, that help make "inner-city people sell food stamps to buy lottery tickets."

When the Texas Lottery started last year, the criticism was tacitly acknowledged. Texas's ad guidelines pointedly state that "advertising should avoid language and visuals that are directed at the economically disadvantaged. For example, claiming that a lottery ticket is 'your ticket out of poverty' is not allowed."

Lottery ads also draw fire for misleading consumers about their chances of winning big. In fact, the majority of lottery ads don't mention the odds against winning at all. A survey by two Duke University economists found only 20% of all lottery ads, and just 12% of radio and TV spots, accurately report the odds. When ads do cite odds, it's usually the odds of winning anything, not the top prize. Thus, a Connecticut TV spot that said the "overall chance of winning is 1 in 30" was technically accurate—but the chances of winning the jackpot were closer to 1 in 13 million.

Recent variations of that theme include the Kansas State Lottery tagline, "Somebody's always winning"; New York's "All you need is a dollar and a dream"; and a Texas jingle that says, "Hey, it's great when you get that winning ticket in your hand / Always knew that you would pick it." And an Illinois TV spot for its Little Lotto game proudly announces that players have "40 times better odds to win" the top prize, without saying what the odds were before or are now. "Play Little Lotto. The odds be with you" is the screen copy.

Critics say ads also propagate the idea that playing the lottery is a smart alternative to sound investing, education or hard work. They cite such examples as an Illinois Lottery spot that showed a player poking fun at savings bond buyers, a New York commercial in which a mother suggested her daughter needn't study hard for a scholarship because the mother is playing the lottery, and a New York City subway poster that read in Spanish, "The New York Lottery helped me realize the American dream."

Wisconsin state Sen. Risser particularly objects to exposing young people to such advertising. "The advertising just whets the appetite of the youth," he says. "It glorifies get-rich-quick schemes, and that's bad public policy."

In fact, much lottery advertising fails the standards of accuracy and fairness applied to private sector advertising, critics say.

"If a private company tried to use the advertising tactics of state lotteries, it would find itself in serious trouble with government regulatory authorities," the Heartland Institute said in its report.

State lotteries escape government reproach because it's the government itself that authorizes the advertising. The Federal Trade Commission, which oversees private-sector ads for games and contests, doesn't monitor state lotteries. In fact, Congress has specifically exempted state-run lotteries from most federal laws regulating such marketing.

The Federal Communications Commission does have a rule banning lottery commercials in states where lotteries aren't legal. Whether that rule stands is now before the U.S. Supreme Court, in an important commercial-speech case in which a radio station broadcasting in North Carolina has sued for the right to carry commercials for the Virginia Lottery. North Carolina doesn't allow lotteries, but the station says more than 90% of its listeners are in Virginia. A federal appeals court last year upheld the FCC rule.

The ad industry's self-regulatory arm, the National Advertising Division of the Council of Better Business Bureaus, also ignores state lotteries.

Not surprisingly, ad executives resort to the same arguments on lottery advertising they have used in the debate over cigarette and liquor ads.

"The lottery passes the two tests—it is a legal product and the advertising is truthful," says John O'Toole, president of the American Association of Advertising Agencies.

"Advertising is not in the business of protecting people from themselves," Mr. O'Toole says.

"Lottery critics want to eliminate lotteries under the mantle of the poor innocent citizen who needs to be protected from himself," he says. "You can't protect people from themselves."

Agency executives and lottery marketers also contend they're very sensitive to upholding the American work ethic in selling the games.

JWT's Patricia Juckett, account director on the California lottery, says its research shows that many of the lottery winners continue working.

"Winners use the money for saving for college or paying off a mortgage," she says, adding that the ad strategy is to depict winners as real people.

"You can never have an ad where you have the ultimate fantasy of walking up to your boss's office and telling him to take the job and shove it," says Ms. Sharp, the state lottery marketing director.

In a carefully crafted recent campaign, New York Lotto ads by DDB Needham Worldwide attempt to skirt the "ultimate fantasy" issue by showing a jackpot-winning mail-room clerk buying the company he works for rather than quitting his job.

It's not unusual to see reality casually flouted in lottery ads. A recent campaign re-created the Old West for El Gordo, a game instituted in Maryland for one month to help boost revenues. The ads portrayed "El Gordo" riding through town doling out bags of money.

DDB Needham's creative team defends the fantasy approach of its clever, award-winning New York Lotto campaign. One TV spot, for example, shows a lottery winner and regular guy being announced—"Bob of Buffalo"—as he enters an illustrious grand ball.

"We're not promising them they're going to win," says Bob Mackle, exec VP-executive creative director. "We're giving them the permission to believe that they could win."

But one DDB Needham ad for the New York Lotto creates a false impression common in lottery marketing. In it, a young man asked what he'd do if he won the Lotto replies, "I'd say, 'Mom, Dad, thanks a million.' And that's exactly what I'd give 'em."

In truth, as is the case with virtually all big lottery prizes, he wouldn't get $1 million in a lump sum but in 20 annual payments whose discounted present value is substantially less than $1 million.

As a matter of strategy, lottery advertising invariably focuses on winning rather than benefits the state receives through lottery proceeds. The reason, advertisers say, is that buyers don't respond to such messages.

Terry La Fleur, a gaming expert and author of *The Compendium of Lottery Statistics*, says: "Players don't buy tickets because they're helping schools. [Playing lotteries is] a very me-oriented objective."

California's Ms. Sharp says highlighting where the dollars go is a Catch-22 situation and can be deceptive.

"We don't want them to think that lottery tickets fund schools because that would be misleading. Lottery tickets only make up 2% to 3% of the education budget," she says.

An Ohio legislator, state Rep. Marc D. Guthrie, has gone so far as to propose a legal ban on mentioning education in lottery ads in that state. Such advertising "creates the perception that the lottery is helping education more than it is," he says. "The public believes that the schools are better off than they are so they vote against tax levies and local property taxes to improve schools."

In fact, critics contend that even the alleged earmarking of lottery revenue for good causes such as schools is deceptive, because legislators simply allocate less to these programs from other sources. The result, in many instances, has been little or no funding gain for the program the lottery is supposedly benefiting. In Florida, to cite just one example, the percentage of total education funding contributed by the state has actually decreased since the lottery was adopted in 1986.

Perhaps most alarming to some critics is that lottery advertising pays scant attention to the problem of compulsive gambling, which experts say is exacerbated by lotteries. The National Council on Compulsive Gambling estimates that 10% of lottery players are addicted to the games. Although some states have 800-numbers on the backs of tickets, directing buyers to Gamblers Anonymous-type organizations, few ads directly address the addiction problem.

Texas Lottery officials discussed creating ads like the responsible-drinking campaigns of alcohol advertisers but have yet to do so. "We considered something like, 'Don't spend more than you can afford,'" a spokesman says.

Some critics note the awkward situation states find themselves confronting. Lamenting the lack of state funding to help compulsive gamblers, the Minneapolis *Star Tribune* recently editorialized, sarcastically:

"And why should the state spend millions to combat gambling evils at the same time it spends other millions on lottery advertising intended to make gambling look like harmless fun?"

For now, more pressing than the issue of misleading advertising to most lottery marketers is how they can juice up their marketing to keep revenues growing. Research shows that interest in lotteries wanes after the novelty wears off, so the games must constantly be repackaged and refreshed. In addition, the recession has crimped consumer spending on lotteries.

Thus, though overall lottery revenues have continued to rise, individual consumers are spending less on the games. In 1992, according to a Gallup Organization poll of 1,007 people over 18 who had played the lottery in the past month, consumers spent an average $28 a month on lottery tickets, down from $53 a month in 1989.

"Our lottery ticket sales have dropped to almost half what they were just a few years ago," says John Christos, owner of Holiday Liquors on Chicago's near north side. "We used to have lines halfway down the block!"

California's lottery was especially hard hit by the state's economic slump and a pullback in advertising.

So lottery marketers, like any other consumer company, must add new products and otherwise find ways to rejuvenate sales. When sales of the big lotto games started peaking in 1991, states began trying new games like keno and even video lotteries. "We're all looking at what the next niche is," says

Pamela Koupal, Kansas State Lottery marketing director. "Maybe it's video lottery."

South Dakota enjoyed a huge jump in ticket sales—to $151 million last year from $21 million in 1989—after it became the first state to offer video lottery machines. These dispense paper tickets rather than coins to winners but are otherwise virtually identical to slot machines.

Lotteries' continued success depends on these new types of "social" games played in bars, restaurants and bowling alleys, marketers say. But these games face some tough going. Several states including New York, Illinois and Massachusetts, have already banned video lottery, and a bill in New Jersey would prohibit adoption of keno without voter approval.

Keno employs on-line video monitors that display winning numbers and prize drawings. Lottery opponents especially decry keno because of the frequency of prize drawings—typically every 5 minutes.

They contend these machines are highly addictive, especially to young people. In an editorial attacking keno, *The New York Times* called it "a compulsive gambler's dream."

New Jersey Gov. Jim Florio has also expressed reservations about keno. In a letter requesting state lottery officials to halt a keno test, the governor said, "It is time for government...to turn its attention to strengthening its understanding of both the role that gambling plays and the interaction among the various forms of gambling."

While some lottery boosters nonetheless see the new games as essential to continued growth, critics like Georgia's Mr. Conkey think they will mean the undoing of lotteries or at least drastic curbs on the way they're marketed.

"The same thing that happened with the liquor industry [restrictions on advertising and sales] is going to happen to lotteries," he says.

In the meantime, advertising remains the essential element of lottery marketing. And advertising promoting gambling will continue to escalate as state governments approve more private gambling activities in casinos and riverboats.

For example, recent ads in Connecticut promoting the establishment of casinos tout them as a "ray of hope" for the state's economy.

As far as the ad industry is concerned, the imprimatur of the states renders moot such questions as those raised by Mr. Conkey and other critics.

"This is not an advertising problem," says Four A's Exec VP Harry Paster. "The moral dilemma has been passed by the states' acceptance of the lottery."

Playing Lottery "Was Relaxing," Until...

What Was Advertised as a Fun Activity Degenerated into Addiction

Iris Cohen Selinger

Tom, a former bank manger, sometimes stumbles over the two large boxes filled with lottery tickets he still keeps in his garage.

"It's just paper," he says. "Very expensive paper."

In dollars, his losses add up to some $75,000, but the boxes also serve as a reminder of other, dearer losses—his job, his wife, his self-control.

Tom, 49, is a lottery addict, though he didn't always know it. At first, he played the lottery for entertainment. In fact, he says he believed lotteries were very much as advertised—a fun, leisure-time activity.

"It was like spending a dollar for cigarettes," he says. "It was money for relaxation. I didn't realize how much money I was pumping into it."

Tom was no high roller. The casinos and the track were too "hard core" for him. Lotteries seemed harmless. He didn't equate them with gambling until later. In the meantime, he comforted himself with the social acceptability of playing.

"I would look at the big ads celebrating the winners. [Lottery promotions] had the governor's name on [them].

"It seemed like a perfectly fun and harmless social activity."

But soon this "entertainment" became a requirement. He rarely went a day without playing.

"I thought, 'You've got to be in it to win it,'" he says, sounding eerily like some of the lottery slogans trumpeted in ads across the country.

Hoping to recoup the losses of the day before, the week before, the month before, he began doubling his bets. When that didn't work, he borrowed from a loan company to cover his losses. He was diligent in repaying the loans on time, so he could renew them. The pattern continued for 10 years.

Then the lies began.

He tried to hide the addiction from his wife by having his loan bills mailed to his office.

His wife found out anyhow.

"My wife said, 'If you take out another loan, you can kiss this marriage good-bye,'" Tom recalls.

It finally caught up with him.

He embezzled $3,000 from the bank that had employed him for 18 years.

He lost his job. His wife filed for divorce.

After years of denying that he had a gambling problem, he had hit bottom. He called Gamblers Anonymous for help.

He hasn't played the lottery in 18 months. He has a new job at the Council on Compulsive Gambling, a counseling group that administers the national 1-800-GAMBLER helpline.

He's in recovery. He's facing the enormity of his losses. He's trying to piece his life back together.

Lottery Ad $ Dilemma

As Need to Advertise Grows, Budget Shrinks

Iris Cohen Selinger

The worst is over, but California offers a cautionary tale of how the recession and the absence of advertising nearly destroyed one of the most successful lotteries in the country.

After reaching $2.6 billion in sales in fiscal 1989, a national record, California State Lottery revenues nose-dived to $1.4 billion in fiscal 1992, which ended last June 30.

Ad spending, tied to projected sales, once totaled a hefty $60 million but plunged to $29 million last year.

Budget constraints forced the state to cease TV advertising from February through June of last year, just when two new games were being introduced that needed heavy launch spending. This further aggravated the sales crisis.

"It's a killer," says Sharon Sharp, California lottery marketing director. "When sales are high, you have more dollars for advertising, but when [they're] not and you really need the advertising to increase sales, there's very little money."

"No other business could run this way," she says.

By law, the lottery's administrative budget, including advertising, is limited to 16% of revenue. Schools get 34% of lottery revenue, and 50% goes to prize winners.

Ms. Sharp previously ran Illinois' lottery and was hired in late 1991 to revive California's floundering business. One of her first moves was ditching ad agency Dailey & Associates, Los Angeles, and after an extensive search, hiring J. Walter Thompson USA, San Francisco.

The new ad strategy focuses on the "freedom and security" that winning a lottery provides, rather than showing winners buying yachts or mansions. Winners "use the money so that 20 years later they don't have to worry about their paychecks," she says.

To support the new advertising and the introduction of games such as keno, Ms. Sharp made a bold and controversial decision to project high sales for 1993, to get more money for advertising.

"There was no other way," she explains. "We were in danger of shutting down."

Ad spending this year will be $31 million, up only slightly from last year. But lottery officials claim they made more efficient media buys this year.

Though short of her projected $1.9 billion, revenues for the year ending June 30 should reach $1.75 billion, a 25% increase from last year.

Sizing Up the State Lottery
Advertising Accounts

Advertising Budget*	Lottery State	Advertising Agency
$8.70	Arizona	Evans Group
$29.50	California	J. Walter Thompson
$6.82	Colorado	Karsh & Hagan
$2.11	Connecticut	Cronin & Co.
$3.90	D.C.	Nagy Films-Jayen Grp.
$1.10	Delaware	RT&E
$1.96	Idaho	Elgin Syler Drake
$20.77	Illinois	Bayer Bess Vanderwarker; Equinox; Tassani
$5.18	Indiana	MAD
$4.90	Iowa	Schreurs & Assoc.; Thomas C. Porter & Assoc.
$2.23	Kansas	Lida Advt.
$6.50	Kentucky	Keynote Comm.; Bandy Carroll & Helige; FS&M; Designing Ideas
$5.58	Louisiana	Bauerlein
$0.75	Maine	O'Nell Griffin & Assoc.
$8.63	Maryland	Trahan, Burden & Charles
$11.60	Massachusetts	Hill, Holliday, Connors, Cosmopoulos
$13.60	Michigan	Bozell
$7.61	Minnesota	Carmichael Lynch
$8.00	Missouri	Valentine-Radford
$0.67	Montana	Fifth Avenue Advt.
$0.84	New Hampshire	O'Nell Griffin
$2.50	New Jersey	CHC
$22.94	New York	DDB Needham
$15.13	Ohio	Marcus Advt.; Forest Grove Advt.

Advertising Budget*	Lottery State	Advertising Agency
$4.80	Oregon	Cole & Weber
$0.54	Rhode Island	Halladay Inc.
$0.43	South Dakota	Media One Advt.
$10.11	Texas	GSD&M
$4.31	Tri-State Megabucks	Pick Three Ltd.
$0.59	Vermont	Communicator's Grp.
$22.02	Virginia	Earle Palmer Brown
$6.20	Washington	McCann-Erickson
$2.80	West Virginia	Fahlgren Martin
$3.29	Wisconsin	Hoffman York & Compton

Grand total: $286 million

*for fiscal 1992 (in millions)
—La Fleur's 1993 World Lottery Almanac

Tricks of the Trade

The Many Modern Ways Casinos Try to Part Bettors From their Cash

James Popkin

U.S. News & World Report, **March 14, 1994**

At precisely midnight on October 11, 1991, an obscure Chicago neurologist slipped behind a row of quarter slot machines at the Las Vegas Hilton and switched on a homemade contraption of cardboard, black metal and old fan parts. For the next 48 hours, the hidden device pumped a pleasant-smelling vapor into the stale casino air.

The neurologist was not an intruder but a scent expert invited to the Hilton by casino manager Lee Skelley to test whether certain smells can subtly influence slot machine players to wager more. Over the next two days, Hilton gamblers poured thousands of quarters into the 18 nearby slot machines—45 percent more than usual for an October weekend.

The days of shaved dice, missing face cards and rigged roulette wheels are long gone. But the pursuit of profitability in the corporate era of gambling has turned the average casino into a financially hazardous place for bettors. In Nevada and Atlantic City, for example, confidential documents reveal that five casinos now pump Chicago neurologist Alan Hirsch's secret scent—Odorant 1—into the slot machine pits 24 hours a day. (The Las Vegas Hilton never took the idea beyond the testing stage.) Some casinos have even studied how the controversial psychologist B.F. Skinner altered the behavior of rats and pigeons. But of all the tricks in the casino manager's Psych 101 handbook, the subtle manipulation of time is by far the most common.

In 1980, a math whiz named Jess Marcum spelled out exactly how time affects a gambler's odds. Marcum, who helped to develop radar and the neutron bomb before becoming a casino consultant, figured that a craps player who wagered just $1 every bet for two months straight would have only one chance in 2 trillion to win $1,000 before he lost $1,000. On the other hand, by decreasing his exposure at the craps table to just 25 minutes and wagering $200 every bet, that same gambler would increase his odds to 1.15 to 1. Even the lowest-ranking casino official knows the concept: Since all casino games give the house a mathematical edge, the longer a player gambles, the greater the house's chance of winning.

That helps explain why gamblers frequently get lost in a maze of slot machines and why down-home gambling halls offer free "Ladies Breakfasts" at 6 a.m., a slow point in the casino day. Over a year, a special promotion or interior-design element that somehow keeps gamblers at play for just five more minutes a night can add millions to a casino's gross, or "hold." The Harrah's Casino spends tens of thousands of dollars a year studying whether fresher air, wider aisles and even back supports on slot-pit stools will make customers comfortable. And slog it out longer, too. "We're now developing technology that's just lighting the felt" on blackjack tables, says Harrah's president, Phil Satre. "We're trying to keep [light] off the forehead of the customers, which is draining on them from an energy standpoint."

Hidden Purpose

Such sensitivity to customer comfort abounds. For example, nearly all new slot machines sold in the United States have built-in bill acceptors. Gamblers like the devices because they no longer have to wait in line for change, and casino managers love them because they keep slot hounds glued to their stools.

Like car plants, casinos also stress productivity. The hidden cameras above the casino floor scan for fast-fingered dealers and card cheats. But the ubiquitous "eye in the sky" also enables casino officials to conduct regular "game-pace audits." At the Aladdin Casino in Las Vegas, blackjack dealers are instructed to deal at least 75 to 80 hands per hour. They are also supposed to shuffle six decks of cards in less than 80 seconds. The reason: Shuffles can eat up eight rounds of playing time an hour. In a year, the Aladdin could earn an extra $1.2 million if its blackjack dealers never had to shuffle.

Penny-pinching casinos set faster production schedules, especially when the nightly cash hold tumbles. "We don't instruct people to deal faster," says Bob Stupak, owner of the Vegas World Casino in Las Vegas. "They better deal as fast as they [expletive] can or they're gonna work someplace else."

Casinos have become pop-psych laboratories. When a player at a low-limit blackjack table flashes a $100 bill and asks for chips, for example, dealers at many casinos are under orders to dole out chips of the lowest-possible denomination. Partly a convenience for gamblers, the practice also is meant to discourage low bettors from pocketing higher value chips when they leave the table. Such players are likely to blow all 20 of their $5 chips one at a time, the thinking goes, but might hold onto a $25 chip and never gamble it away. "Psychologically, casinos don't want gamblers to realize how much they're losing," explains one Atlantic City dealer.

But slot pits are the true training grounds for casino mind games. Deep, dark colors like black, red, purple and blue trigger a strong response in slot players, research shows. So, slot machine manufacturers like IGT, based in Reno, Nev., prominently feature those hues. IGT North American President Bob Bittman says research also shows that gamblers no longer associate winning with the cherry and plum symbols on many slot machine reels. Poof, they're gone. "Fruit is a dinosaur. Ninety-nine percent of the machines we sell now will not have fruit," Bittman says.

Some casinos go to even greater lengths to exploit gamblers' subconscious preferences. Casino consultant David Britton says that after surveying dozens of Nevada-based slot players he confirmed a hunch that they are drawn to bright-red machines. But after several minutes, the players subconsciously tire of red and seek softer hues. Since casinos want to avoid "transitional periods," when players leave one machine in search of another, Britton devised a new system where players are now lured to the brightly colored machines at the end of a long row of slots. But the machines closer to the middle of the row feature softer colors, like blues and greens.

Sometimes casino operations look to actual psychology for inspiration. In 1966, University of Nevada undergrad Larry Andreotti was studying Skinner, one of the first scientists to demonstrate how positive reinforcement can influence animal behavior. Andreotti told his father, the late Rome Andreotti, who at the time was one of the rising stars on the operations side of the growing Harrah's chain. "A lot of the behavior I saw in the lab seemed comparable to the control one has over behavior in casinos," explains Larry Andreotti, who today is a college psychology professor and Skinner specialist in Canada.

Smart Rat

In 1937, Skinner taught a white lab rat named Pliny to operate a rudimentary slot machine. After Pliny pulled a chain with its teeth, a marble would fall. The rat would then drop the marble in a slot and receive its reward, 1/20th of a gram of a dog biscuit. By tracking Pliny's reactions over time, Skinner learned that the rat became more motivated when he got a biscuit only occasionally, and randomly. Pliny would drop even more marbles into the slot, in other words, when he was not sure when the biscuit would fall next.

Rome Andreotti applied Skinner's findings to the casino. If most slots were set at about the same payout rate, recalls a former Harrah's president, Richard Goeglein, Andreotti would slip in a few machines with a much more generous jackpot percentage. The casino wouldn't indicate which machines offered better odds, but gamblers soon learned that there were a few ringers in the crowd. And the search for those machines sent gamblers into a Pliny-like, quarter-dropping frenzy. "Rome knew how to reward people for continual, consistent play," says Goeglein.

Coincidentally, slot machine makers have also put Skinner's theories into practice. Modern slots reward players with frequent, small payoffs—often as inconsequential as one quarter—that entice gamblers to keep chasing their dream. Thirty years ago, by contrast, small, frequent payoffs were unheard of, says slot machine historian Marshall Fey. The new payout system works. "It's like eating popcorn. It's very hard to stop playing," says Jeffrey Lowenhar, senior management consultant with the Resorts casino in Atlantic City.

One firm took gambler manipulation too far. In 1986, Universal Distributing began selling slots that produced "near miss" combinations. Instead of running randomly, the slot reels often stopped so that players could see the symbols of a payout just above or below the pay line, giving the false impression that gamblers had missed a massive jackpot. Although the machines quickly became a hit with customers and slot managers, Nevada gaming authorities outlawed the near-miss illusion in 1989.

It was a Sunday afternoon, and Pennsylvania jewelry salesman Sam Roberts was bellied up to a roulette table at his favorite Las Vegas casino. Dressed in what he described as his "Mr. T starter set"—three gold necklaces, four gold bracelets, a gold watch and four gold rings—Roberts seemed to epitomize the successful Vegas man about town. When asked whether he was ahead after three days of roulette, Roberts said he wasn't "paying any attention."

But the casino certainly was. On a computer screen just off the casino floor, the file on Sam Roberts (not his real name) was extensive. Not only did it reveal his exact losses on his current trip ($2,092) but it had already figured his average bet ($20.88), time spent gambling (11 hours and 39 minutes) and "average worth," or how much Roberts should lose ($528) based on time and the house's 5.26 percent edge at roulette. It also contained personal data like Sam's height (5'10"), weight (300), hair color (brown)—even whether he needed corrective eyewear (yes).

Casinos amass personal information to enhance customer service and reward steady players with "comps"—complimentary meals, show tickets and hotel stays. (They never reveal internal data, although Roberts agreed to for this article.) But there's a hidden agenda. Casino marketers need detailed histories to keep old customers loyal and, more important, to "capture" new ones.

If marketers learn, for instance, that divorced slot players from Cleveland who love boxing lose big and often, the casino will buy mailing lists and try to find sucker clones. Gamblers who can be lured to the hotel are especially prized. "If we can get you to stay in our hotel we can bump up your average trip worth," one marketer says. Everyone gets in on the hustle. When a casino hotel is nearly full, reservationists will scan the computer and open remaining rooms only to known gamblers with a high trip worth.

A decade ago, most casinos bothered to gather data only on high rollers. Now they use slot-club cards to snare the meat-and-potatoes guy, too. After filling out a survey and receiving an ATM-like card, slot junkies insert them into a "reader" built into almost all slot machines. In a distant computer room, casinos track the action 24 hours a day, down to the last quarter.

Giveaways

Players who use the cards the longest get the most comps, somewhat like a frequent-flier giveback. At the Trump Castle in Atlantic City, an internal document shows that 64 percent of all slot players now use the Castle slot card. The cardholders lost $109 million to the slots last fiscal year, or about $101 per player per trip. Slot players who never bothered with the card, by contrast, lost $31 per trip on average.

For an industry governed by odds, casinos leave little to chance. To line their pockets just a wee bit more, they've added games with stunning house odds. Many casinos now offer "double-exposure blackjack," for example, in which the dealers reveal all their cards; players keep trying to top the dealer's hand without going over 21. Novices fall for the ruse, overlooking the rule allowing the house to win all ties. "That one rule change is worth about 8 or 9 percent in favor of the house," explains Arnold Snyder, editor of the *Blackjack Forum* newsletter.

Many riverboat casinos also offer "multiple-action black-jack," with complex rules that encourage gamblers to place three bets on every hand. "It causes players to play dumb and put more money on the table," Snyder says. If gambling critics can be believed, that neatly sums up the danger of America's latest entertainment craze. As any old Vegas hand will tell you, "If you wanna make money in a casino, own one."

Hustling Without Any Guilt

Kevin Horan
U.S. News & World Report, March 14, 1994

Bob Stupak, Las Vegas's most controversial casino owner, once used a tic-tac-toe-playing chicken to lure gamblers to his casino and, in an unsuccessful bid for mayor, mailed voters free "stock certificates" that could be traded for drinks. His comments provide insights into how some casinos operate.

On greed: "We target everybody. That's the business I'm in. Money's money. What's the difference if it's a Social Security check, a welfare check, a stock dividend check?"

On slot machines: "When we put 50 machines in, I always consider them 50 more mousetraps. You have to have a mouse-trap to catch a mouse."

On gambling "entertainment": "You can't disguise this industry. You can put clown uniforms on...you can have Streisand, but it is what it is. It's our duty to extract as much money from the customer as we can. And send them home with a smile on their face."

On superstition: "For 20 days in a row, my crap pit lost money. After five days, I changed the dice manufacturer. After 18 days I bought new tables and burned the old ones. Put new tables in, new dice, new stick, new dealers. All the praying in the world isn't gonna change your luck."

On alcohol: "Benny Binion [late owner of Vegas's Horseshoe] used to say, 'Whiskey is the greatest gambling tonic in the world.' Although everyone else in town was pouring a three-quarters shot, he used to say to give them a shot and a half. He was right."

Anatomy of a Casino

Almost every element in a casino conspires to keep gamblers there longer and to separate them from as much of their money as possible. The mazelike architecture, fast dealers, bartenders and even hotel clerks are in on the hustle.

Eye in the sky: Overhead cameras prevent cheating but also help casinos make sure dealers work fast.

Baccarat: At private baccarat pits, most big casinos still hire attractive women called "starters" to get the high-roller action going. These fancy shills play with the casino's chips, which they never cash.

Body language: At empty tables, dealers stand with their hands at their sides, never crossed. It's a welcoming gesture that pulls players in.

The big wheel: The money wheel is a vestige from carnival days. Fittingly, it offers lousy odds, giving the house a minimum 15 percent edge.

Lights—Aroma—Elvis: Casino lighting creates a dazzling atmosphere in which night is day. But it can't be too bright or gamblers will tire—and possibly walk away. Fresh air keeps gamblers going, too. So cool, clean air circulates every eight minutes or less. A few casinos also pump in fragrances, which supposedly increase slot machine revenues. Cheap buffets and entertainment keep people inside.

Slot machines: Slot managers often place low-denomination machines by the entrance, like a store hawking its sale items in the front window. Casinos and slot machine makers study which colors attract gamblers most; deep reds act like a magnet.

Roulette: "Muckers" scoop up losers' chips to prepare quickly for the next spin.

Time is money: Dealers must keep games moving, dealing 60 to 75 hands per hour in many casinos and shuffling six to eight decks in less than 80 seconds. The more hands that are played, the better a casino's chances of winning, since the odds always favor the house. If casino profits dip, some pit bosses ask dealers to quicken their pace. If casinos can persuade gamblers to trust robotic shuffling machines, dealers can constantly deal—earning casinos millions of additional dollars.

Hotel reservationists: When a casino hotel is nearly full, clerks decide who can stay there based on each gambler's "average worth"—how much he's predicted to lose.

Frequent-gambler cards: Slot players insert them in the machines to "win" free meals and rooms. They trigger a computer that records all play—handy for marketers.

Dollars and drinks: Booze loosens gamblers up. Many casinos pour a hefty shot and a half. Check-cashing booths and credit card machines abound, and it's often easier to get casino credit than to get a car loan. Instead of giving you an option, most casino ATM machines spit out a single $100 bill when you request $100.

Part VI
Picking Shallow Pockets

Lottery promoters go to great lengths to point out that middle class people spend more in total on tickets than poor people do. But those numbers are deceiving. When broken down another way, figures often show that poor people play more often and spend a greater portion of their incomes when they play, making lotteries an extremely regressive way to raise cash.

Study after study bears this out. "In California, the poor spend 15 percent more of their income as a percentage, on lottery tickets than the rich do," wrote Paul Karr in a 1992 Portland, Maine *Casco Bay Weekly* article. "A Detroit study showed that, in tough times, middle- and upper-class folks stopped playing the lotteries—but poor urban dwellers kept right on playing." Oregon State University professor Daniel J. Brown surveyed more than 3,000 Oregon residents in 1990 to find out who played the lottery the most and why. He found that the poor "commit a greater proportion of their household expenditures to the lottery" and that "education is negatively related to lottery play and generally is the best predictor of the amount of play." Clearly states are taking advantage of their most vulnerable citizens.

And the Poor Get Poorer...

Lower-Income Communities Spend Larger Share of Their Money on Lotteries

Ford Fessenden and John Riley
December 4, 1995
Newsday, Inc. Copyright © 1995
From the Series "Gambling: The New National Pastime"

"Pursue your dreams within your means." So reads one of the New York State lottery's slogans. And it reflects an agency that prides itself on its appeal to the hopes and aspirations of the regular guy. Not rich. Not poor. Average. "Our consumers sit in the middle," says lottery director Jeff Perlee.

But the numbers paint a different, and more complicated, picture. They say the lottery draws far more from people in the state's poorest neighborhoods than in its wealthiest ones. They say those of modest means spend a dramatically higher percentage of their income on the lottery than do the rich. And they say that as New York's annual lottery sales spiral above $3 billion, the state is relying on a revenue source that takes from lower-income households to a far greater degree than the primary way the state raises money—the income tax.

Those were the key findings of a computer-assisted *Newsday* study that examined both geographically coded lottery sales data from the past three years and a complete list of ZIP codes of one million prize winners. Coming at a time when growing lottery revenues and advertising budgets and the start-up of Quick Draw keno have sparked increased debate over the lottery's role, the study showed:

• As a proportion of their income, lower-income families spend vastly more than middle-income or wealthy families on the lottery. Annual lottery spending per $10,000 of household income was eight times higher in the lowest income areas than in the highest. Even in a middle-income range—between $40,000 and $50,000 a year—lottery spending as a proportion of household income was nearly 2 1/2 times higher than in the $75,000 to $100,000 income range.

•Statewide, some of the lowest-income neighborhoods—in places like the South Bronx and Harlem—had higher spending per household than some of the highest-income areas, such as Great Neck and Scarsdale. In ZIP codes with an average household income of under $20,000, lottery spending averaged $35 a month per household, while in ZIP codes with an average income of over $100,000, spending averaged about $29 a month per household.

•On Long Island, discrepancies in lottery spending can be especially stark. In Mill Neck, one of Long Island's richest communities, lottery spending is only about $17 a month per household. In Hempstead town, where the average income is about a third of Mill Neck's average, spending is $81 a month. In Huntington, average spending is $35 a month per household, while in lower-income Wyandanch, spending averages $63.

•Compared with the income tax, which taxes the wealthy at higher rates than the less affluent, the lottery takes a greater share of money from those with lower incomes. Households making less than $30,000—about 29 percent of the households in the state—paid only 9.66 percent of income tax in 1992, the most recent year available. But census tracts with median income of less than $30,000 accounted for about 33 percent of lottery sales.

•Early data from the lottery's controversial new Quick Draw keno game indicate that it could worsen regressive aspects of the lottery by appealing—to a greater degree than other games—to players in low-income areas. While Lotto, the most popular game, sells best in census tracts with a household income above the state average, sales of Quick Draw during its first six weeks of operation were highest in census tracts with an average household income far below the state average. Areas with high Quick Draw sales also had lower education levels and [higher] minority population than areas where other games sold well and the state as a whole.

Overall, New York State's lottery sold $3.02 billion in tickets last year. Forty-eight percent of that was returned to players as prizes, and 41 percent—$1.24 billion—went into state coffers to pay for education aid to localities. The rest—$323 million—covered the lottery division's administrative and marketing costs. Lottery sales are expected to rise to $3.5 billion this year and, boosted by full implementation of the new Quick Draw keno game, could approach the $4 billion mark next year.

Experts said *Newsday*'s overall results were consistent with findings in other states. While lotteries indeed attract the broad public participation lottery officials point to, the games differ from most other consumer products—like cars, food or movies—because the games draw as much or more money from the poor as from the rich.

"What other product can you think of that is like that?" said Philip Cook, a Duke University economist who co-authored *Selling Hope*, a 1989 book on lotteries. "Lotteries suggest this is a very democratic thing, very appealing, and that's true. But from the point of view of simple financial concerns, poor families are spending a much higher percentage of their income that would only be incidental for a rich family. That's what is normally missing from the lottery's account."

The findings also came as no surprise in lottery outlets in lower-income neighborhoods. At Chance Liquors on Merritt Avenue in Wyandanch last week, Alton Toomar, 38, paused to explain why he was buying a fistful of Win 4, Take 5 and Pick 10 tickets despite being unemployed with three kids to support—and to explain why the poor need the lottery more than the rich do.

"We don't have anything and we're trying to *get*—legally," Toomar said. "I'm looking for my lucky break like everyone else."

Such comments, according to those who have studied lotteries, are typical. "As you go down the income scale, people perceive it as a form of investment," said Robert Goodman, a professor at Hampshire College in Amherst, Mass. who studied the U.S. gambling industry for two years under a Ford Foundation grant. "As you go up the income scale, people do it as a form of entertainment. Government is promoting an activity that is essentially a poor form of investment for most people."

Critics of the lottery quickly seized on *Newsday's* findings as new evidence that Quick Draw—contrary to the assurances of Gov. George Pataki and lottery officials—would not appeal to an "upscale" audience, and that the lottery generally is doing more harm than good by preying on the poor.

"The state lottery has blinders on," said Sen. Frank Padavan, a Queens Republican who fought the introduction of Quick Draw. "They have no reason in their minds to be concerned about anything except maximizing public participation in the games they promote. The entire picture is one of the state of New York contributing a variety of social ills and economic harm to a significant portion of the population that can least afford it."

Other legislators said the findings renewed long-standing concerns about the lottery's regressivity, but they lamented their inability to give it up as a revenue source.

"They get those people who most need divine intervention in their plight, and the chances of that are so ridiculous," said Denny Farrell, a liberal Manhattan Democrat who chairs the Assembly's Ways and Means Committee. "But what am I going to do? Raise the subway fare another five cents?"

Defenders of the lottery said that, even if it draws money disproportionately from the poor, it has the great benefit—unlike taxation—of being voluntary. "Each individual still has a choice of whether they want to participate," said David Gale, executive director of the North American Association of State and Provincial Lotteries. "If lotteries go away, then the revenue has to come from somewhere and those people will have no choice. If taxes are raised, the people will have to pay the taxes."

And many lottery players say they don't want government to protect them from themselves. "I'd rather be a volunteer," said Grace Rogers, a 50-year-old state government worker playing Quick Draw at Arcade Stationery in Wheatley Heights last week. "We all could find better uses for our losses. But it's fun—you can come in, spend your money and laugh about it."

State lottery officials said they believed lottery spending is somewhat lower among both the very poor and the very wealthy but well-distributed among other income groups. The officials challenged the validity of *Newsday's* study of lottery-sales data—a methodology used only to reach conclusions about the Quick Draw game. Both methods used by *Newsday* produced essentially the same overall picture of a regressive lottery system. And Charles T. Clotfelter, another Duke researcher and Cook's co-author, said the total approach provides an accurate portrayal.

Because people don't necessarily buy lottery tickets where they live, New York lottery director Perlee said, conclusions drawn by matching sales data with income characteristics of the areas in which sales are made can be skewed by different commuting patterns of rich and poor and high-selling lottery outlets in commercial areas with only a small number of residents.

These problems "present such a large statistical variable as to render any conclusion concerning a correlation between lottery sales and income of a given area insupportable," Perlee said.

The sales-data approach used to analyze Quick Draw was adjusted to exclude census tracts with small populations and areas with large commuting centers, like Penn Station. Perlee, however, said that, aside from methodology, Quick Draw locations are still being added, and it is premature to draw conclusions about who is playing.

"It's much too soon to tell," he said.

Lottery officials, in their annual report, say the typical active lottery player is 43 years old, has an average household income of $49,850 and is more likely to be female than male. Also, 95 percent of players are high school graduates, and 63 percent have had some college. That relatively upscale portrait comes from an annual market survey of households with income over $15,000.

The survey fails, however, to take into account households with incomes of less than $15,000. In a separate study of low-income households conducted this year, the lottery division found lower participation among low-income households. Nevertheless, the study found that 46 percent of households under $15,000 had played the lottery in the preceding month. Had those figures been included in the lottery's portrait of the average player, the average income the agency calculated would have been lower. That survey, unlike *Newsday*'s study, also didn't look at variations in the amount players at different income levels spend on the lottery. But the lottery's own survey indicated spending might be higher at low-income levels.

It showed, for example, that antes in games vary dramatically based on income. While the under-$15,000 group had played Lotto far less than those with higher income during the month preceding the survey, a higher percentage of the poor had played the lottery's two daily numbers games—New York Numbers and Win 4. Those two games, the lottery survey found, attract the highest average player spending per month— $76 and $70.80, respectively—while Lotto attracts $24.14 a month from the typical player.

In one sense, experts cautioned, the lottery's dependence on spending by the less affluent plays an insignificant role in the overall state revenue. The money the lottery contributed to state coffers last year represented just 2.74 percent of the $42.4 billion the state raised through taxes, fees and the lottery.

But that number is inching up. In fiscal 1992, it represented only 2.27 percent of the total. In the current year, lottery proceeds—swelled by the start-up of Quick Draw—are budgeted to provide 3.38 percent of all state funds. Without the lottery, the state sales tax would have to rise three-quarters of a cent to make up for the lost revenue.

Critics say that growth, combined with other changes in the state's tax structure, raised concerns about undue burdens on the poor.

The reduction of top income tax rates under Gov. Mario Cuomo beginning in 1987, and the tax cut sponsored by Gov.

George Pataki this year, have combined to make the income tax itself less progressive, according to Frank Mauro of the Fiscal Policy Institute, a labor-funded Albany think-tank that specializes in studying state finances.

At the same time, those cuts have put a greater burden on less progressive taxes—such as the sales tax and the property tax. Given the lottery spending patterns identified in *Newsday*'s study, Mauro said, the poor are losing three ways: "Too many of us have ignored the regressivity of the lottery and concentrated on the income and other taxes," he said. "The lottery can be worse because it tempts those most in need. While the lottery is a small part of the big picture, it's an extremely regressive part."

A Lottery Primer

Kathy Kmonicek

Newsday, Inc. Copyright © 1995
From the Series "Gambling: The New National Pastime"

Lotto. Players pick six numbers out of 54 on a Lotto ticket. There are two games for a dollar. Drawings are twice a week, on Wednesday and Saturday nights. Getting all six numbers correctly wins the jackpot, a minimum of $2.5 million. Players can also win lower cash prizes by matching three, four or five numbers. Thirty-eight percent of the sales is allocated as prize money. Odds of winning first prize: 1 in 12,913,583, winning 50% of prize money. Overall odds of winning 1 in 333.

Take Five. Select five numbers from 39 on a betting slip. The minimum play is one game per dollar. Drawings are twice per week on Tuesday and Friday nights. Getting all five numbers wins the jackpot, usually about $300,000. Players can win lower amounts by matching three or four of the numbers. Matching two numbers wins a free ticket. Fifty percent of the sales is allocated as prize money, with first prize getting 20 percent. Odds of winning first prize: 1 in 575,757. Overall odds of winning 1 in 8.77.

Pick 10. Players pick 10 numbers from 1 through 80 on a betting slip, with a minimum play of $1 for one game. Drawings are every night, with 20 out of the 80 numbers selected. First prize is $500,000 for matching 10 of the 20 selected numbers. Players can win lower amounts by matching 6 to 9 of the numbers. Matching none of the numbers wins $4. Odds of winning first prize are 1 in 8,911,711. Overall odds of winning are 1 in 17.

Numbers. Players pick a three-digit number and choose one of nine different ways to play, from matching the exact numbers and order (called a straight bet) to matching only the front pair or the back pair. Drawings are once a day, with a minimum bet of 50 cents. The maximum payoff is $250 for a straight bet, which also has the highest odds of winning, at 1,000 to 1. The odds of getting the front or back pair are the best, with 100-1 odds.

Win 4. Players select four numbers, and as in the numbers game, decide on one of 13 different ways to play, ranging from a straight bet to various combinations. The minimum bet is 50 cents and drawings are every day. The odds of winning the first prize in a straight bet are 10,000 to 1. The payoff for a 50 cent play is $2,500. The easiest odds are for combinations, at 417-1.

Quick Draw. Bettors decide how many numbers they want to play and pick up to 10 from a field of 80. Players can also decide how much to bet per game and how many consecutive games they want to play. The lottery's computer picks 20 numbers from the field of 80 and displays them on a monitor. There are 158 drawings every day. Players can win $100,000 for playing and matching 10 of the numbers in a $1 bet. Lesser amounts can be won for matching five numbers and up. Matching no numbers yields a $5 payoff.

Instant Games. The lottery has at least 10 games in which a player scratches off a play area to match scores, get bingo numbers, or reveal slot machine symbols. One of the most popular instant games is Win for Life, in which the top prize is winning a $1,000 a week. The odds of finding a card that gives those winning markings are 1 in 7,560,000. The overall odds for the scratch-off games are about 1 in 5, including lesser cash amounts and free tickets. Some of the state's games are: Win for Life; The 100,000 Game; Bingo; Lucky 7s; Magic Money; Black Jack; Instant Slots; On a Roll; $2 Bingo; and Deuces Wild.

Income and the Lottery

In New York State, people with lower incomes are more likely to buy lottery tickets. Here's a breakdown of income levels and lottery spending compiled from ZIP code and census data.

Avg. household income	Annual household lottery spending per $10,000 of income
Less than $20,000	$234
$20,000—$29,999	$146
$30,000—$39,999	$116
$40,000—$49,999	$113
$50,000—$59,999	$96
$60,000—$74,999	$81
$75,000—$100,000	$46
More than $100,000	$30

Part VII

Over the Edge

The Cost of Compulsive Gambling

By pushing lottery play and trips to the casino, states and casino owners are pushing a growing number of citizens over the edge; people like Jean Mott, written about in the following Minneapolis *Star Tribune* article by Norman Draper. A 39-year-old mother of three, Mott's gambling habit got so out of hand that she pulled a ski mask over her head one day and robbed a convenience store to support it. Compulsive gambling has increased dramatically in states where gambling has been legalized; there were twice as many problem gamblers in Minnesota in 1994 as there were in 1990. According to the National Coalition Against Legalized Gambling, "In Iowa, the legalization of casinos more than tripled the addiction problem. A study released in July 1995 found that 5.4 percent of the state's adults [roughly 110,000 residents] are lifetime pathological or problem gamblers," compared to 1.7 percent before riverboats came to the state.

Compulsive gambling leads to crime, bankruptcies and lost wages: Some estimates put the social cost of each compulsive gambler at more than $50,000 a year. Robert Goodman, author of *The Luck Business*, estimates that the suicide rate for compulsive gamblers is five to ten times higher than it is among the general population. In covering the macabre trend, the *Reno News & Review* recently reported five suicides in six weeks: Three men and one woman jumped from the tops of downtown casino parking garages and one jumped from a casino hotel room. By blanketing people in pro-gambling rhetoric, politicians and casino moguls are driving people to desperate ends.

Mom's Gambling Habit Drove Her to Robbery

Norman Draper
Star Tribune, July 10, 1995

Meet Jean Mott.

She's a 39-year-old wife and mother of three. She works as a secretary at a machine tool shop in Savage. She likes pizza and went to a Roman Catholic school as a girl. And like many moms, she just took her 14-year-old daughter to get braces.

But there's another side to Jean Mott. She's a compulsive gambler. And now, a convicted felon.

During two years of heavy gambling at Mystic Lake Casino in Prior Lake, Mott made a shambles of the family's finances, and even pawned her wedding ring, to support her addiction to slot machines and gaming tables.

But that's nothing compared to her latest caper. In January, desperate over her gambling losses, Mott pulled a ski mask over her head and robbed the Brooks Superette convenience store in Shakopee.

"I did something terrible, and I'm shocked that I did it," Mott said as she sat in the living room of her Shakopee home with her husband, Dan, 42, and daughter Kristina, 14.

"It was a shock, but it wasn't a shock," said Kristina, turning toward her mother. "I could see you needing to do it, but I couldn't imagine you doing it."

Mott wanted to tell her story in the hope that others with gambling problems would seek help in time.

"I don't want anybody to go through what I went through," she said.

Mott was picked up by Shakopee police the day of the holdup. She pleaded guilty to robbery, and served 20 days in Scott County jail. She also was sent for 30 days to a gambling addiction treatment program in Granite Falls, Minn. For another month, she had to wear a locked electronic ankle bracelet so she could be monitored 24 hours a day. She could go to work from 7:15 a.m. to 4:45 p.m., but otherwise couldn't leave home without permission.

Mott certainly isn't the first person driven to extremes by gambling. Plenty of other citizens have piled up mountains of debt, embezzled from employers and even robbed banks to support their gaming habits. Indeed, gambling obsessions are now viewed as addictions, with treatment programs and organizations tailored to deal with them.

Mott had never committed a felony before the robbery. She attributed it to the gambling, but doesn't want to use it as an excuse.

"It's true that the gambling is why I did what I did," she said. "But it was wrong. It was against the law…I don't want somebody to say, 'She didn't get punished because she had an addiction.'"

There are few clues in Jean Mott's past to explain the gambling problems or the robbery. There was a divorce and some serious bickering between Kristina and Dan, who is her stepdad. Mott has a fondness for beer that led to a six-pack-a-night habit until she quit right before her second marriage. She's a heavy smoker, and Dan had noted on their occasional gambling forays that it was tough to pull her away from the slot machines and gaming tables. That's about it.

The heavy gambling started a couple of years ago.

Mott had a good cover. She had the graveyard shift at the Kmart distribution center in Shakopee that ended at 7:30 a.m., and often left early without pay if her job was done. Mystic Lake was a straight shot south on County Rd. 83. Dan would head for work at 4:30 a.m., and Mott would gamble at least three nights a week.

Sometimes she stayed over well into the day, asking Kristina to stay home from school to look after her youngest daughter, Brittany.

"She'd call me up and say, 'I'm at the casino; do you want to stay home from school?'" Kristina said. "I'd always have to make up these little lies, like that I was sick, had strep throat, was throwing up."

Kristina already knew about her mother's gambling habit by then.

"She basically let me know because she borrowed money from me," Kristina said.

As the casino guzzled the family earnings, Mott pawned her wedding ring, the VCR and the television, pretending that she needed money for other things. Eventually, she told Dan.

"I told her that if she did it again, she's out the door," he said. But the gambling continued. Mott asked her mother for money and used her to get loans to feed her habit. On Dec. 7, Mott swallowed about 40 Tylenol tablets in an attempt to kill herself. Still, the gambling went on.

A month after the suicide attempt came the nadir of Jean Mott's life. She had gone back to the casino and blown another paycheck, which she was supposed to give to her mother for safekeeping.

"I didn't know what to do,"she said. "I drove around for, like, three hours...I drove by the [Brooks Superette] store and thought it would be easy to rob it...I'd just go in there and say, 'Give me all your money,' just like in the movies." She drove home to pick up a ski mask and some duct tape and returned to the store at 5 a.m.

"I was scared," she said. "My heart was beating 100 beats a minute." She got out, put the ski mask on and went into the deserted store with her hands shoved in her pockets. She told clerk Gerald Gessell to open the cash register and empty the cash in a bag. After a shaky effort to bind Gessell's hands and feet with the tape, she fled the store with $233, and drove around for a while, tossing the ski mask out the window.

"Then I went to the casino again," she said. She wasn't hard to catch. A suspicious police officer had written down her license plate number when he saw her car parked near the store that morning, then followed her. Later that day, police made the connection between the car and the robbery, and an officer came by for a visit. After a feeble effort to deny any knowledge of the robbery, she confessed.

Ironically, Mott's victim used to work at Mystic Lake Casino. And he had been robbed before, in 1977, when he was a clerk at a 7-Eleven store in Minneapolis and a robber pointed a sawed-off shotgun at him.

"This one was probably a little bit easier," Gessell said. "I think it's probably different when you see a gun."

Gessell said he harbors no hard feelings or bitterness, but he doesn't have much sympathy either.

"I'm not one who really thinks gambling is a problem," he said. "I think a lot of people just use that for an excuse."

After the robbery, Mott got her job at the machine tool shop. She likes that it's a day job, which would make it harder to sneak off to the casino should the urge strike again. She said she thinks the jail time and treatment program helped. It's also helped that her family has stayed together, she said.

Mott has noticed that other cravings seem to be taking the place of the gambling. She's "eating like crazy," and puttering manically around the house. There's also the smoking habit, too, up to two packs a day.

But will the pull of the casino ever prove too strong to resist?

"I guess I really don't know," she said. "I think doubts are there. I think they will always be. But I feel like it won't happen. When I think about it, it kind of makes me sick to my stomach."

Addiction

The Dark Side
of the State's Gambling Boom

By Susan Lampert Smith and Ron Seely
Wisconsin State Journal, **March 21, 1993**

When Jim started going to Gambler's Anonymous meetings in Green Bay more than two years ago, he'd sit alone in a meeting room in the Fox Valley Hospital and wait. After a few weeks, his lonely vigil ended. Another problem gambler showed up to commiserate.

But today—with a greyhound track and several tribal casinos within a convenient drive of everyone in the Fox Valley—loneliness is hardly a problem at the hospital's Gambler's Anonymous meetings. Now the meetings are attracting 20 regulars, and another 100 or so who stop by now and then when their gambling habits become troublesome. There are now four meetings a week instead of one.

Addiction is the dark side of the Wisconsin gambling boom. It is one of those things sometimes described, often by gaming proponents, as a "cost" associated with legalized gambling. That, however, seems a coldly indifferent way of describing an illness that can so darken lives.

Mary Zavalydriga, a pit boss in the Golden Nickel Casino near Wisconsin Dells, recalls a day last August when she had to search the casino for the parents of a child who had been left in the parking lot in a car. The mother and father were found inside, plugging slot machines.

Numbers documenting the extent of compulsive gambling in Wisconsin are difficult to come by. The state's gaming commission is just now searching for an independent research firm to study both the positive and the negative impacts of gambling in Wisconsin.

But Walter John Chilsen, a senior policy adviser to the commission, said that study won't be ready for months. Voters in next month's gambling referendum will have to rely mostly on statistics from other states and the stories of addiction that are already surfacing in Wisconsin.

In Minnesota last year, gamblers lost $300 million at the state's 15 tribal casinos. They lost $660 million in all forms of gambling in the state including the tribal casinos, pari-mutuel betting, lotteries and charitable games.

Like Wisconsin, Minnesota has seen a rapid expansion in gambling. And Steve Coleman, a state planner who keeps track of gambling-related statistics, said a soon-to-be-released report on gambling impacts will show evidence that the number of addicted gamblers has also grown in the last year. Calls to a state-run hotline for Gamblers Anonymous doubled during 1992, Coleman said. Six state-financed treatment centers for problem gamblers and family members were opened last year and four of them are at capacity; several have waiting lists.

Studies by the University of Minnesota showed the number of adolescents with gambling problems also increased, from 2.9 percent in 1990 to 3.5 percent in 1992. Other studies showed evidence that Indian adolescents and adults are more likely to be problem gamblers than non-Indian peers and that problem gambling is affecting poor families at twice the rate of the general population.

Even now in Wisconsin, with most casinos entering their second year of operation, experts say there could be as many as 50,000 people addicted to gambling in the state. Clinics around the state specializing in treatment of gambling addiction report increasing numbers of clients. It is, the experts say, a deadly addiction which, if unchecked, can lead to shattered families, psychiatric disorders and suicide.

The American Psychiatric Association defines compulsive gambling as "a chronic and progressive failure to resist impulses to gamble, and gambling behavior that compromises, disrupts, or damages personal, family, or vocational pursuits."

But beyond these numbers and words are the stories, stories of shattered lives that are already surprisingly easy to find in Wisconsin.

Jim, who uses only his first name in the tradition of self-help group members, has been a compulsive sports gambler for 35 years. But he said that most of the new members have been laid low by the newer forms of legalized gambling, especially the video gambling offered by local Indian tribes at casinos and even at gambling gas stations. .

"We're seeing a number of them," Jim said, "people who haven't gambled in the past" who got involved after the legalization of the state lottery, dog tracks and the Indian casinos. Most, he said, are "mesmerized" by the video gambling machines.

He said he has met an elderly couple who are in danger of losing the home they owned free and clear before they started gambling. He said they couldn't accept GA's philosophy of abstinence because they still thought they could win back their money. "We tried to tell them that even in the extremely unlikely event they got their money back, they wouldn't keep it," Jim said.

John Cowan, pastor at Shawano's Community Baptist Church, said he's counseling more people than ever before for gambling-related problems. In the past 10 years, he said, he recalls working with three families because of gambling problems. In the last year alone, during the rapid expansion of several northern casinos, he's working with six families. He's seen broken marriages, lost homes, huge and unmanageable debts. "What we're having to deal with here is the destruction of families," Cowan said.

Dave Barrett, the priest at St. Michael's Catholic Church on the Menominee reservation near Shawano, said he's seen a growing gambling addiction problem among tribal members. He said he's also seen growing problems related to gambling—increasing drug and alcohol abuse, for example.

The vast majority of people who gamble—probably 97 to 99 percent of them—can limit themselves and gamble for entertainment, said Dr. Michael Goldstone, director of Bellin Psychiatric Center's addiction program in Green Bay. "You have to keep it in perspective when you're looking at the other ills of society," Goldstone said, saying that while 1 to 3 percent of the population are likely to become addicted to gambling, 8 to 15 percent will fall victim to another legal vice, alcohol. But for those who are drawn into complusive betting by the chiming slot machines and the thrill of "easy money," the future looks grim. Statistics, Jim said, show that complusive gamblers who don't quit end up insane, in prison or dead.

"It's not funny," said Jim, who plans to vote to limit gambling on April 6 although GA itself takes no position on the issue. "Five of our members have attempted suicide and another one is in prison."

Staggering Debts Can Grow Quickly and Quietly

Chris Ison
Star Tribune, **December 3, 1995**
From the Series "Dead Broke"

Thousands of Minnesotans are burying themselves in debt because of gambling, borrowing millions of dollars they'll never be able to pay back.

Hundreds are filing for bankruptcy protection. Hundreds more are avoiding bankruptcy but dragging themselves and their huge debts to credit counseling services. And hundreds or thousands more are keeping their problems private, financing their gambling habits through personal loans, cash advances on credit cards and bad checks, and at pawnshops that have sprung up around casinos across the state.

It's a trend that has gone largely unnoticed. State government has mostly anecdotal information about people in debt, and there have been no comprehensive studies about the scope of the problem.

Yet bankruptcy lawyers, credit counselors and others have begun to recognize the effects emerging over the past three years, since the state's largest casinos emerged as such dominant entertainment destinations.

The gambling culture has sent a steady flow of gamblers into federal bankruptcy court, a number estimated at more than 1,000 a year, according to interviews with attorneys and bankruptcy court officials and reviews of bankruptcy records.

And a *Star Tribune* analysis of bankruptcies indicates that the debt is huge. "Compared to 10 years ago, there are 20 times as many people who have gambling debts," said Jack Prescott of Minneapolis, perhaps the state's most well-known bankruptcy attorney.

In Chapter 13 federal bankruptcies—where people agree to pay back a portion of their debts—about 5 percent of the cases being filed are at least partly related to gambling, according to estimates by the trustee's office and cases reviewed by the *Star Tribune*. That's 213 out of about 3,900 new cases filed every year.

Hundreds more are filing Chapter 7 bankruptcies and not paying back a penny of their debts. No one knows how many are filing at Chapter 7, partly because trustees don't help the debtors set up a repayment plan, so they know less about what caused the debt.

But the actual number of bankruptcy filings is much higher than the 213 estimated by the Chapter 13 Trustee's Office. Attorneys representing two of the largest bankruptcy practices in the state estimate that as many as 20 percent of their cases are related to gambling, a trend that has developed just in the past several years.

Many gamblers have obtained 10 or 15 credit cards—some more than 20—and have withdrawn their limit in cash advances, which they can't pay back. Some run up more than $100,000 in debt at high interest.

They are people like Patricia Nelson, a 54-year-old, semi-retired widow from Savage who may never dig out. When Nelson's husband died in 1989, he left her $100,000 from a life insurance policy and a lot of lonely nights. She started spending those nights at Mystic Lake Casino in Prior Lake, and the $100,000 in the video poker machines.

By last month, she had gambled away the $100,000 and another $40,000 from a second mortgage on her house. She then ran up another $45,000 in debt, most from cash advances on 10 credit cards.

It happened $20 at a time. The poker machines could turn a $20 bill into 80 points, which seemed like a lot of points and just a little money. Until the $20 bills started to add up.

"That's all you think of it, is 80 points," Nelson said. "You don't think of it like it's $20 and you can buy a pair of shoes with it.

"I'd think that's all I'm spending, and I'm going home. And it never happened that way."

And then there are the more well-known, influential people like Hennepin County Commissioner Sandra Hilary of Minneapolis. She filed for bankruptcy protection last year, two days after admitting that she was addicted to slot machines. She estimated that she had lost nearly $100,000 gambling.

Pawnshops Prosper

It's impossible to know just how many people are in debt because of gambling. In most bankruptcy cases, people don't have to say why they're in debt.

But those gamblers who have been identified in bankruptcy proceedings and at credit counseling agencies provide a glimpse into the huge debt that is being amassed by Minnesotans.

Curtis Walker, a Twin Cities bankruptcy attorney, said he handles about 100 cases a month, and he estimated that 20 percent are gambling-related. That's 240 a year from one lawyer alone.

There are many more in debt who don't file for bankruptcy protection.

Credit counseling services, many of which discourage clients from filing for bankruptcy protection, are finding gambling at the root of many of their clients' troubles.

At two large services, 10 to 15 percent of the clients have obvious gambling problems, said credit counselors who recently reviewed their client base at the request of the *Star Tribune*. The two services together—Consumer Credit Counseling in Duluth, which has 10 offices around the state, and The Village Financial Services in St. Cloud—are seeing problem gamblers at a rate of about 90 per month, or more than 1,000 per year.

And with the emergence of more casinos over the past five years, at least 17 new pawnshops have sprung up near them, where gamblers hock their possessions for far less than their real value to support their gambling habits.

In Cass Lake, population 923 and 4 miles from Palace Casino and Bingo, there are three new pawnshops and an old one just outside of town. That's a pawnshop for every 231 people. There are now three pawnshops in Cloquet, population 11,055 and neighbor to Black Bear Casino.

One pawnshop owner in Cass Lake said that more than half of the shop's customers are gamblers.

"We have our drinkers and our gamblers," said the owner, who asked not to be identified.

At the Pawn Broker in Mora, about 20 miles from Grand Casino Hinckley, owner Mona Lingen said gamblers make up about 20 percent of her business.

"You can spot it right away. They need big money, and they need it right away," Lingen said. "And then they buy [the merchandise] back. And eventually, it gets 'em. They get into you too far, and they can't get out."

In the middle of the interview, Lingen took a call from a customer. "That was a guy that just lost his ass at the casino," she said after hanging up. "He needs $1,000. He just paid me back $2,500 yesterday."

Average Owed: $40,000

Talk to the pawnbrokers, the bankruptcy attorneys and the credit counselors, and a bleak picture emerges. Then look at the bankruptcy filings, and the extent of the financial devastation can be shocking.

"We've noticed this to beat hell, ever since this phenomenon of casino gambling came in," said Prescott, the bankruptcy attorney.

His office handles about 3,000 bankruptcies a year, and he estimates that 10 to 20 percent of them are gambling-related. That's 300 to 600 cases per year from just one law office.

Add that number to attorney Walker's filings, and there have been 500 to 800 gambling-related bankruptcies every year from two lawyers alone.

Walker notes that many gamblers might have gone bankrupt sometime even without the gambling losses. But gambling clearly increases the debt and speeds up the process for many. And it is a main cause of bankruptcy for others.

J.J. Mickelson has seen the trend close up. Mickelson, the Chapter 13 trustee for the U.S. Bankruptcy Court in Minnesota, started keeping track with an informal system about two years ago.

When he finds a bankrupt gambler, he marks the file "G-7/11." He recently produced a list with 68 such cases, and his counsel, Steve Cresey, identified others. But they acknowledge that they probably identify only a third of the actual gambling-related cases that go through their office.

In an attempt to draw a profile of bankrupt gamblers, the *Star Tribune* identified 105 bankruptcy cases clearly involving gamblers. The cases show:

•The average bankrupt gambler owes more than a year's salary in unsecured debt. The average debt—usually not including the mortgage and often not car loans—is more than $40,000. The average salary is about $35,000.

•Those numbers suggest that problem gambling is mostly a middle-class problem. But not totally. The debtors range from unemployed or retired people with little or no income, to white-collar business people making more than $50,000 per year.

•Most of the debt is on credit cards, and the numbers are huge. The average person or family had eight cards, although many had 10 or 15 cards. Two people had 25 cards each—all Visas, Mastercards or Discover cards. One had 29 cards. And the large debts on each card indicated the gamblers had taken out cash advances of $5,000 to $10,000 or more on each credit card—and couldn't pay it back.

•The amount of admitted gambling losses among the 105 totaled more than $1.1 million, though half of those in the sample either didn't know how much they had lost or didn't admit any losses. The average loss for those who provided estimates was $22,000 per person or family. If that number held true for those who didn't designate losses, the total losses for the 105 cases would total $2.3 million.

And if Mickelson is right that that's just a third of the actual cases, then gambling losses among Chapter 13 bankruptcies alone would total nearly $7 million since mid-1993—around $3 million per year.

•Creditors are losing big money. Of the approximately $4.2 million in debt, the 105 debtors will pay back about 40 cents on the dollar, or about $1.69 million. That means creditors will be out more than $2.5 million. Experts say that consumers probably pick up much of that tab indirectly, in higher fees and interest rates on credit cards.

•Many gamblers don't pay their taxes. Of the cases analyzed, 23 percent owed federal taxes averaging more than $4,000 each. Twenty-one percent owed state taxes averaging more than $1,600 each.

Gamblers Easy to Spot

Gamblers' cases often stand out in bankruptcy court and at credit counseling services.

Gamblers have higher numbers of credit cards, more debt from cash advances on credit cards and often more personal loans. Many have bounced checks at the casinos.

"Their debt often includes things of significant legal consequence, probably more often than we see with other debtors," said Jodi Anderson, a counselor with Consumer Credit Counseling Service in Duluth. "Bad checks very often. We have quite a few compulsive gamblers who've stolen money in one form or another…We see a lot of personal loans. They tap into anybody who'll give them money.

"The low-income gamblers, all of their necessary living expenses are way behind. Their rent, their utilities. They've received shut-off notices. They've gone to pawnshops. Folks who have more resources, we see a lot of credit-card advances."

Prescott has seen it over and over.

"We're finding it's just too easy for them to lose all their money and then go out into the hall and get money with their credit cards," Prescott said.

And Jeff Copeland has done it over and over.

Copeland, 21, used to get his $500 paycheck, take $100 in cash and head to Little Six Casino in Prior Lake, the predecessor of Mystic Lake.

"I didn't want to take more money, so when I [ran out] I'd have to go home," he said. "But then I'd get out there and I'd get more money...Because I'm a totally different person when I'm at the casino."

He often withdrew the rest of his paycheck at the casino's ATM. The next day, he'd get an $800 advance on his credit card. "And I'd put it in the bank and it's like I never gambled. I'd think, 'There, my cash is back in the bank.' And it would only take a week and I'd go right back. And it went on and on and got bigger and bigger. And before I knew it, I was over my head."

By this summer, Copeland was $20,000 in debt.

"I probably won't even be able to go to college now. It's just not feasible because I don't have the money. I have to have two jobs just to pay off my debt."

Cash Readily Available

Like Mickelson, Prescott and others, Copeland believes the easy availability of cash at casinos feeds gambling addiction. Copeland said he might have been saved had ATMs and services that provide cash from credit cards not been available at the casino.

There are few incentives for casinos to regulate the availability of credit to gamblers. The casinos don't lose because they don't give the credit—they simply make the money.

The credit card companies—there are now more than 7,000 card issuers—have made record profits in recent years despite increasing bankruptcy nationwide. Interest rates are so high—they average 18 percent, according to one industry watchdog group—they more than make up for losses from bankruptcy. And the issuers pass much of the loss on to the consumers, through higher rates, fees and penalties, said Ruth Susswein, executive director of Bank Card Holders of America, a nonprofit credit-card education group.

"They're making so much money it's been worth it to them to keep offering credit," Susswein said.

Most casinos also rent space to companies that cash checks and provide credit-card advances for fees. A Twin Cities company, Game Financial Corp., provides a glimpse into the millions of dollars in cash issued at the casinos.

Game Financial started business in 1991. By the end of 1992, it was doing business in four Minnesota casinos. From just the fees for credit-card advances and check cashing at those four casinos, the company reported revenues of $1.7 million that year.

By the end of last year, the company operated at 10 locations nationwide and reported revenues of more than $5 million. Today, it operates at 26 sites.

There is no limit to how much cash a gambler can get through such services. The company once cashed $30,000 in checks for a customer over a five-day period, said marketing director Louis Dachis.

And many people cash checks they can't cover.

"I don't think it's something we want to disclose, but we get a good number of checks back," Dachis said. "I wouldn't say it's more than half, but we do get a good number back."

Gambling's Grim Toll

Chris Ison
Star Tribune, December 3, 1995
From the Series "Dead Broke"

In less than a decade, legalized gambling in Minnesota has created a broad new class of addicts, victims and criminals whose activities are devastating families and costing taxpayers and businesses millions of dollars.

Many are people who had never previously broken the law, but who turned to robbery, forgery and embezzlement to support their habits.

Thousands have ruined themselves financially, and a handful have killed themselves. Thousands more will live for years on the edge of bankruptcy, sometimes working two or three jobs to pay off high-interest credit-card debt.

They are mostly middle-class people, whose appetite for wagering grew from the office football pool or church bingo to pulltabs, racetracks, lotteries and casinos when state and federal governments began legalizing them in the mid-1980s.

They are people such as 19-year-old John Lee, a St. Paul college student who lost $8,000 in two nights at Jackpot Junction Casino near Morton, Minn. He returned home that second night, kicked down the door to his apartment, put the barrel of a shotgun to his head and killed himself.

They are people such as Lam Ha of Blaine, a father of two and waiter at a restaurant. Last year, he and his wife filed for bankruptcy protection with a $76,000 debt, much of it on 25 credit cards. They listed gambling losses of $40,000 in 1994 alone—more than their joint annual income.

They are people such as Reva Wilkinson of Cedar, who is in federal prison after she embezzled more than $400,000 from the Guthrie Theater to support her habit. In addition to the money she stole from her employer, her case cost taxpayers more than $100,000 to investigate, prosecute and adjudicate.

And it will cost taxpayers millions of dollars more for crimes committed by gamblers throughout the state, especially in counties that are home to or near casinos, where crime has increased far faster than elsewhere in Minnesota, according to a statistical analysis by the *Star Tribune*.

Crime is just a small part of the total cost to Minnesota. Even conservative estimates of the social costs of problem gambling suggest that it costs Minnesotans more than $200 million per year in taxes, lost income, bad debts and crime.

Today, gambling is as socially acceptable in Minnesota as a night at the movies and as commonplace as Little League baseball. An estimated $4.5 billion is legally wagered in the state each year.

And while most Minnesotans gamble for recreation and suffer no ill effects, the number of problem gamblers has multiplied as the industry has flourished. Ten years ago, there was one Gamblers Anonymous group meeting in the state. Today, there are 49.

The estimated number of people who have experienced significant problems because of gambling doubled from 1990 to 1994 and now exceeds 100,000, according to two independent surveys conducted last year. One of those studies also concluded that there are about 38,000 "probable pathological" gamblers in the state—people with serious gambling addictions.

Political Leaders Silent

Political leaders—even those who have taken an interest in gambling issues—acknowledge they know little about the problem. There has been no comprehensive study of the social costs—the debt, crime and suicides associated with problem gambling. The state doesn't know what kind of treatment works, or how successful the programs it funds have been. Experts can't even agree on a definition of problem gambling.

Several officials have pushed recently for better studies of the socioeconomic costs of legalized gambling, citing the lack of good research that has kept public agencies from spending more money to treat compulsive gambling. In fact, the Legislature this year reduced the amount it spends to treat gamblers.

"The social costs really haven't been assessed very accurately, and they certainly haven't been quantified at this point," said Assistant Attorney General Alan Gilbert, a member of the state Advisory Council on Gambling. "But I think common sense tells you that there has to be some adverse effects...We know that's there, we just don't know the extent of it. And I think at this point in time, we need to determine that if we can."

For years, Minnesota has touted the economic benefits of its gambling boom—often using the industry's more benign term, "gaming." And clearly, there have been benefits.

Indian communities, which own 17 casinos statewide, are building schools, clinics, roads and businesses. Pulltabs have allowed charities to make millions of dollars for worthy causes. The State Lottery raises millions for the state's general fund and an environmental trust fund. And thousands of people gamble and win prizes every day without becoming hooked.

But at what cost? The state doesn't know, and so far has chosen not to find out. When members of the Advisory Council on Gambling met this summer to consider funding a study of the socioeconomic costs of gambling, they decided such a study would be too costly and might be unreliable.

Meanwhile, the Legislature has debated whether to allow bar and restaurant owners to put slot machines in their businesses, and then take a cut of the profits. And the state spends $8 million a year advertising for the lottery. That's nearly eight times the amount it spends on efforts aimed at helping problem gamblers, including treatment, education, a compulsive-gambling hot line, research and other efforts.

On the federal level, the issue of gambling addiction only recently started to generate action. This fall, committees in the House and Senate held hearings on bills that would authorize a national commission to study the economic and social effects of legalized gambling.

The gambling industry acknowledges the problem of addiction, but stresses that it involves a tiny percentage of gamblers. Some casinos contribute money to treatment programs, and some require their employees to undergo training to identify problem gamblers so they can suggest that they get help.

Marsha Kelly, spokeswoman for the Minnesota Indian Gaming Association, said 95 percent of gamblers don't have problems. She noted that the country doesn't "eliminate driving because 60 percent of our people don't wear seat belts."

Gambling, Kelly said, "is like any other industry. It's got a downside, and some people are going to be more vulnerable than others. The industry has a responsibility to address that downside. And that's what they've done here in Minnesota."

Many Problem Gamblers

If there's one thing for sure about gambling studies, it's that nothing about them is for sure. But here are several indicators of the scope of Minnesota's gambling problem:

More gamblers are going bankrupt. There is evidence that more than 1,000 people a year are filing for bankruptcy protection in cases involving gambling losses, according to estimates by bankruptcy attorneys and the bankruptcy trustee's office, and cases analyzed by the *Star Tribune*. Of 105 gambling-related bankruptcies analyzed by the newspaper, the total debt exceeds $4 million, with average gambling losses exceeding $22,000 for each debtor. The average debt was more than $40,000.

Gamblers are committing suicide. Through interviews with police, medical examiners and counselors, the *Star Tribune* found that six people with gambling problems had committed suicide, five of them in the past two years. At least 140 gamblers have attempted suicide, according to interviews with directors of the six state-funded gambling treatment centers.

Seventeen pawn shops have opened near casinos in the state. Several owners said they get 50 percent of their business from gamblers.

Credit counselors are seeing increasing numbers of gamblers with seemingly insurmountable debt. At two large counseling services, 10 to 15 percent of the clients—more than 1,000 per year—have obvious gambling problems, according to credit counselors who recently reviewed their client base.

Minnesotans are burning up welfare payments at casinos. Currently, $39,000 a month in welfare benefits from Hennepin and Ramsey counties is being withdrawn from automatic teller machines in casinos. In September, there were 769 withdrawals of public-assistance benefits at cash machines at Mystic Lake Casino in Prior Lake.

Calls to the state Compulsive Gambling Hotline doubled from 1992 to 1994, reaching nearly 500 per month.

By last year, more than 100,000 adults in the state had experienced "increasing negative consequences" from gambling, a category considered one step away from becoming a true pathological gambler, according to a study by the Center for Addiction Studies at the University of Minnesota-Duluth (UMD). That's 3.2 percent of the state's adult population. And it's double the number from a study four years earlier, just as casinos had begun to emerge as a dominant form of entertainment in the state.

The same study estimated that nearly 38,000 Minnesota adults are probable pathological gamblers, a number that has held relatively steady since 1990. But experts in the field said problem gambling is progressive and that some of the 100,000 problem gamblers of today are likely to turn up as pathological gamblers in the next survey.

A *Star Tribune*/WCCO-TV Minnesota Poll last year found that 128,000 (4 percent) of adults in the state showed signs associated with problem gambling and gambling addiction.

The potential for gambling addiction among youths—the most vulnerable group—is worse, many experts agree. The UMD study found that 4.1 to 6.3 percent of teenagers in the state have experienced problems related to gambling.

"We're going to have our first generation of kids who grew up during a time of legal gambling, and we don't have a clue what's going to happen to them," said Bill Bergwall, senior counselor with the Compulsive Gambling Program at Fairview Behavioral Services in Minneapolis.

Many experts believe that the number of problem gamblers is underestimated, because many gamblers—especially those surveyed by telephone, such as those in the Minnesota Poll and the UMD study—may hide some of their gambling problems.

For example, in the Minnesota Poll, only one respondent among the 803 adults interviewed acknowledged having sought treatment for a gambling addiction. Yet about a third of all respondents said they know someone with a gambling problem, and 8 percent know someone who has been treated for problem gambling.

Experts, therefore, are careful not to place too much significance on the myriad studies of problem gambling. And the lack of confidence in society's understanding of the problem has weakened efforts to squeeze out more public dollars for treatment and education.

"We really don't know how much problem gamblers cost society," said Henry Lesieur, editor of the *Journal on Gambling Studies* and a criminal justice professor at Illinois State University in Normal, Ill. "What we know is it costs a lot of money. It's in the hundreds of millions of dollars. Whether it's $100 million or $500 million doesn't make much difference.

"To me, what's important is, once one person commits suicide or two people commit suicide, those numbers don't make any difference."

Computing Social Cost

Even the most conservative estimates indicate that the social costs are much more than $100 million in Minnesota.

Researchers have tried, through various methods, to establish a social cost for each pathological gambler. The results have differed widely, ranging from $13,200 to $52,000 per gambler.

One of the most conservative analyses, by Robert Goodman, a professor at Hampshire College in Massachusetts and author of the book *The Luck Business*, puts the cost at $13,200, acknowledging that that's probably at the low end.

He used data from other studies, including lost income from gamblers who lost their jobs, costs of prosecution for their crimes and "bailout costs"—money they were given by friends and relatives to cover gambling and living expenses.

To come to a total social cost, Goodman suggests reducing the estimated number of problem gamblers by 40 percent to account for those who have quit—temporarily or permanently—or reduced their gambling significantly. Using the estimated 38,000 probable pathological gamblers in Minnesota, the number is then reduced to 22,800.

The Annual Cost to Minnesota: $300 Million.

Now take Goodman's estimate of social costs per gambler and reduce it even more, to $10,000. The annual cost still would total $228 million.

And that doesn't include any costs for the estimated 100,000 "problem gamblers" in the state. It doesn't include such factors as lost productivity at work, the cost of divorce, criminal acts that aren't prosecuted and suicide.

Researchers in Wisconsin, which has 17 casinos, came up with a similar estimate of social costs using similar methods. The Wisconsin Policy Research Institute reported this year that gambling in the state produces $160 million to $456 million in social costs each year.

Intangible Costs

There are many costs that can't be assessed.

They include the cost of lost education for Jeff Copeland, a 21-year-old from Brooklyn Center who can't go to college because he's accumulated a $20,000 gambling debt. "It ruins your life," he said. "And people don't really understand. I thought about...suicide. It's the easiest way to get out of it."

There's also a cost for spouses and children who quietly suffer as a partner or parent struggles with gambling addiction.

Divorce, domestic violence and neglect are common in families with gambling problems, said Bergwall.

"You see a lot of this lashing out, and then there's the remorse that follows," he said.

And many believe that such problems are on the rise. "We keep on legalizing more and more and more gambling," Lesieur said. "It doesn't take a rocket scientist to know the problems have got to increase."

Conclusion

Due to issues like compulsive gambling, crime and lost jobs, citizens around the country are organizing to keep casinos and other forms of legalized betting out of their neighborhoods. Small business owners have become outspoken, complaining that gambling institutions steal money from their pockets: One newspaper account from a few years ago gave restaurant owners in Florida, Massachusetts and Rhode Island full credit for defeating proposals to legalize gambling in their states. Some legislators have recently begun to oppose gambling as a money maker as well and have made moves to further regulate the industry. According to a July 1996 *New York Times* story, lawmakers are pulling in the reins on lottery advertising. "The Massachusetts state legislature has taken among the most drastic steps, slashing the lottery's advertising budget from $12 million a few years ago to $400,000 this year," the paper reported.

Perhaps the most well-known anti-gambling organizer in the country right now is Tom Grey, head of the National Coalition Against Legalized Gambling. He's garnered a lot of media coverage as the frontman for what he calls the most organized and widespread group fighting gambling in the nation, a group of over 5,000 people from all points on the economic, political and religious spectrums. NCALG takes partial credit for the national study on gambling mandated by Congress in 1996, which promises to be the most comprehensive look at the industry in decades. And Grey, a minister by training, can tick off other victories one after another, all the while pointing out that gambling initiatives can be defeated by popular effort. The David and Goliath nature of the fight only appears to stoke his enthusiasm: In 1995, he says, more than a dozen casino companies were pushing to legalize riverboat gambling in Richmond, Virginia. He says they'd spent somewhere around $800,000 on lobbyists and ads, yet community members "armed with the facts" were able to defeat the initiative. "I thought I'd do this for three months," Grey says, "but then I extended it to six months. I started in October 1992 and it's now October 1996 and I'm still doing it. I've been in 26 states since the beginning of the year. Every time I've gone it's been by invitation."

Since 1994, casino expansion has slowed to a trickle. Grey gives his organization and other citizen activists credit. "We've shifted the discussion from morality to a question of economics and impact on a community's quality of life," he says. "They couldn't stand up to that. They've been selling snake oil and we've been saying, 'Read the ingredients.'"

For More Information on the Battle
Against Legalized Gambling

The National Coalition Against Legalized Gambling
110 Maryland Avenue NE
Washington, DC 20002
1-800-664-2680 or 202-54-NCALG

The National Council on Problem Gambling
P.O. Box 9419
Washington, DC 20016
1-410-730-8008

Gamblers Anonymous
P.O. Box 17173
Los Angeles, CA 90017
1-213-386-8789

John Warren Kindt
Department of Business Administration
University of Illinois
350 Commerce West
1206 South 6th St.
Champagn, IL 61820

Earl L. Grinols
Department of Economics
University of Illinois
483 Commerce West
1206 South 6th St
Champaign, IL 61820

Robert Goodman, author of *The Luck Business*
United States Gambling Research Institute
245 Main Street
Northampton, MA 01060

Index

N

About the Author

Jennifer Vogel is Online Editor at *City Pages*, an alternative weekly newspaper in Minneapolis. In 1991, before graduating college, she won the *Nation* magazine's I.F. Stone award for student investigative journalism. Since then, she's won numerous awards for investigative reporting and feature writing. She lives in Minneapolis.